Stopping to Smell the Flowers

Everything's Coming Up Roses

Stephanie Malo

 FriesenPress

Suite 300 - 990 Fort St
Victoria, BC, V8V 3K2
Canada

www.friesenpress.com

Copyright © 2019 by Stephanie Malo
First Edition — 2019

All rights reserved.

No part of this publication may be reproduced in any form, or by any means, electronic or mechanical, including photocopying, recording, or any information browsing, storage, or retrieval system, without permission in writing from FriesenPress.

ISBN
978-1-5255-4718-8 (Hardcover)
978-1-5255-4719-5 (Paperback)
978-1-5255-4720-1 (eBook)

1. Body, Mind & Spirit, Mindfulness & Meditation

Distributed to the trade by The Ingram Book Company

Table of Contents

Preface	v
We Don't Claim the Land, We Belong to It	1
This Time by Choice	5
Choices	9
On Following Your Dreams	11
Time on My Hands	13
Stopping to Smell the Flowers Isn't Always Easy	15
A Break from the To-Do List	17
The Wind	19
The Chair in the Woods	21
The Funny Thing About Being a Parent	23
Practice Paying It Forward	25
No Regrets	27
Keep Your Vacation with You All Year Round	29
Comfort from Books	33
One Foot in Front of the Other	35
Facing the Stuff as Time Moves On	39
Blinking Lights	41
Barbeque and Meditate	43
On Being Happy	45
Purpose	47
The Library	49
Retracing Your Roots	51
Life Coming to a Halt	55
Teaching Fear by Accident	57
The Cottage	59
Content	61
On Letting Go	63
Light in the Darkness	65
Take Time Out	67

Evolving	69
The Jog of My Life	71
The Art of Being Present	73
Spread Your Wings	75
Right Where We're Supposed to Be	77
Talk to Me, Honey Bee	79
Sure, I'll Go	83
Blessings Raining Down	85
Imprints	87
The Baby Shower	89
The Sounds of Silence	91
Don't Look Back	93
We All Have a Book in Us	95
Keep on Marching	97
Little People Love	101
There Is a Place	103
Unless	107
Acceptance Brings Peace	109
We All Have a Story	111
Society	115
Observations in the Bushes and Other Life Lessons	117
The Flight	119
The Frog and the Filing Cabinet	121
My Shadow	123
Keep on Believing	125
In Stillness We Find Life	127
Rise	129
The Dance of Life	131
Acknowledgments	133
Categories	137
About the Author	141

Preface

Just like with *Stopping to Smell the Flowers: Extraordinary Observations of Everyday Life*, *Everything's Coming Up Roses*, the second book in the Stopping to Smell the Flowers series should be read slowly. Savour each story and give yourself time to reflect on what the story means to you. Each story is shared because of its universalness, its ability to connect us all, and its glimpse into how we're all the same. You can flip through the book and see what story you land on … maybe you're supposed to read that one first. There's also an index at the back that groups the stories into categories so you can choose one based on how you're feeling or where you might need direction or healing. No matter how you read it, I hope that it brings you peace and a little closer to your truth.

We Don't Claim the Land, We Belong to It

I wave my hands in front of my eyes and watch the sun reflecting off my skin, almost making them look foreign to me. I'm on holidays and somehow am the last person remaining in the water. I look at all there is to see beneath the surface, my swim mask snug over my nose and eyes. A quiet commentary goes on in my head as I pretend to film my own underwater adventure series. I reach down and grab a small stone embedded in the solid sand on the bottom. A slow puff of sand particles gently rises up and then falls back into place again. I think to myself that I should collect every rock that catches my attention in order to somehow preserve the feeling of utter freedom I have while doing this, but I don't. The few rocks that I do collect (as many as I can hug closely as I swim back to shore) change colour as they dry, losing their initial sparkle or deepness. One that I do keep—and cart all four hundred and twenty kilometers home, not including the two-hour ferry ride—is one that I have to loosen with my feet, as that's easier than diving down and trying to wrestle it loose. It's a huge chunk of light-pink quartz, and it will sit on a display shelf in my bedroom to remind me that some things are worth digging for, that holidays are important, and that we're all still kids at heart.

The coffee shop at our holiday destination not only makes the most delicious coffee ever, but also sells handmade chocolates in small, clear bags, so you can see that they look like the colourful rocks on the beach. Ranging in colour and size, the biggest chocolate rock is maybe the size of a quarter, and the smallest just less than a kernel of corn. They come in blue, beige, red, and brown, just like you'd see along the shore, except you can eat these ones.

We happen to spot people from our hometown while perusing the small local shops. They tell us that they've visited this place every year since their daughter was little, which would be over twelve years now. They feel the place is spiritual. I share that we do the same things and visit the same places every year, but you never know what part will be your favourite until the journey is done and you're back home reflecting.

It's a similar feeling with friendship. The friend we visit when we vacation here, I've known for twenty-five years. As time ticks by and with each sporadic, or at least yearly, visit, we see how each other's lives, environment, and focus change, if only slightly, and yet how we remain the same.

My husband and I had a similar relationship with our neighbour. We felt an easiness with him, and often words weren't required. We'd just sit on the back deck, taking in the evening. Time stood still, yet the spirit of our friendship stayed the same. All the while we aged physically, got creakier and wrinklier, and the kids grew up.

Waiting for the ferry ride home from our vacation island, we meet Shawn. My husband had called me over to the water's edge because he'd spotted a mink. By the time I get there, the mink is gone.

"His name is George," Shawn says.

Shawn is fishing off the pier and looks to be about twenty-five years old. We become friends, if only for thirty minutes. We learn everything we'd ever want to know about fishing and life on the island. He used to live in the big city and then moved up to the island to help his aging grandparents. His grandfather has since died, but there's no way he'd move back now. The island has him—hook, line, and sinker. His job at the ferry is seasonal, but he also enjoys wood splitting and other odd jobs on the side. He's so easy to talk to … or rather, listen to. He moves from one subject to another with the ease of a skater moving from one skate to the other, and we listen. He remarks that we probably enjoyed the clear water on our holiday. Apparently, the clear water is a sign of unhealthiness. Some water creature was introduced to the system and eats all the microbial life meant for the fish to enjoy, resulting in less fish in the waters.

Once on the ferry, we walk to the front of the boat. As the big ship heads past the loading dock, we see Shawn. We wave and he gives us a big, salute-type wave back, sending us off back to where we're from, and glad to have met us.

On the ferry ride home, a First Nations man gives a drum demonstration. He shares the history of pow wows, explaining that his people are honoured when others come to visit and witness the ceremony. He starts to play the drum and sing, and my son gets the giggles from the high voice followed quickly by the low voice of the singer. When my son gets the giggles, I often can't help but laugh myself. This time I'm so enthralled by the sound, I just let my mind drift away from the present. When the song finishes, the man waves his small drum stick in a full circle motion. Upon completion of the circle, he points at my son in the audience and says, "We also honour the gift of laughter."

We don't claim the land, we belong to it. What is now is also "then," in the past, and "there," in the future. The physical changes, but the spirit is steady.

This Time by Choice

He had been the hardest one to catch. I'd camped out in the driveway for about two weeks in order to get him. I remember sitting under my neighbour's overhang as it rained, a few drops intermittently bouncing on my head and some in my teacup. Looking back, I now know this allowed me to spend some last, precious moments with my wonderful neighbour before he passed on two months later. We'd sometimes sit together in silence on his back deck, covered by a roof that protected us from the elements, just taking in the moment.

The little kitten I'd later name Gerry was determined to stay outside. He wouldn't be persuaded by the tantalizing piles of food we were leaving for him at the back of a live trap that was designed to close the door behind him, or in the cage that would need to be manually shut. I'd even bought a fishing net with a pole on the end, thinking I'd put food out in the driveway and catch him from above, but Gerry was too lightning fast for all those tricks. Every now and then, Gerry would climb up on my neighbour's lap, and I wondered why he didn't grab him and put him in the cage. He said he didn't want to scare him, so he planned to wait a little longer until the kitten got more comfortable. When he admitted that he'd miss the little kitten's friendship once we caught him, I did worry a little. What if my neighbour had no intention of catching him?

We caught Gerry a week or two later—or rather, my neighbour did. For some reason, it was one of the most beautiful things I'd ever seen. The way he caught him was so gentle and kind, it brought tears to my eyes. Gerry had been on my neighbour's lap enjoying a massage, and all that was required was a little nudge, some gentle fumbles almost with a rolling action, and bit by bit Gerry's cute, furry body was guided by fingers old and slow and thick with arthritis into the carrying cage. My cunning ideas and traps had been no match for this lightning-fast creature. The slow, loving, methodical way of my eighty-six-year-old neighbour was what worked. Gerry had no idea of our loving intentions while trying to catch him with food and traps. No idea that it would be his safest, warmest, happiest bet. It took a relationship to develop first. It took trust and patience for him to have a better life.

A year later, when I hadn't seen Gerry in over a day, I realized he must have escaped. As you can imagine, my thoughts jumped to the conclusion that I wouldn't be able to catch him again. I asked around. The kids hadn't seen him with the other cats early in the morning waiting for their treats. Had he gotten out? All four of our cats are indoors only, and everyone is always careful to shut doors quickly behind them. My neighbour was the one who caught him in the first place, not me, but he was long gone.

I was on my own, and I already felt defeated. If he'd gotten out, I figured my chances of catching him were slim to none. I also felt rejected. Even though I was fully aware that Gerry was an animal and would naturally try to escape if he got the chance, I felt that I just couldn't win. You try to do something good, but maybe it's just not what's right. Maybe Gerry would prefer a life outside. It might be a shorter life, but maybe he was willing to take that risk. I was defeated and deflated, so I did what I usually do when I feel that way: I call up to God, or the universe, or whatever higher power or goodness that exists (that anyone can just tap into if you just stop and listen). I asked, "What should I do? Should I let him go, or should I try to catch him again?" Just as I asked the questions, I drove by a billboard with a picture of a cat sitting next to a can of tuna. I couldn't believe my eyes. *What are the chances of that?* I knew I needed to at least try.

I started by going outside and calling his name. That resulted in nothing—not a sound, just silence all around me. I attempted this for a while, going outside and calling his name and then going back inside. At least I was letting him know I cared. I'd almost given up for the day when I looked out the dining room window and saw Gerry lounging in the driveway, all spread out in an obvious state of bliss. He was surrounded by the next batch of homeless kittens, born right where he was born the year before. (Unfortunately, we never managed to find the mother … or the father, for that matter.)

Our eyes met. He seemed happy and proud, as if he'd returned home. Again, I felt rejected. Didn't he like the home we'd opened up to him? Maybe he really wanted the life of natural freedom.

I checked on him through the window periodically, wondering how he was faring. Eventually, I looked and he wasn't there, and neither were the kittens. Curiosity got the better of me, so I went outside to find him sitting comfortably perched on the wooden fence top. I brought out our big bag of cat food and shook it, trying to tantalize him, as he'd been outside for almost two days now. Still nothing. He just stared at me. I went back inside, giving up for a second time. It had gotten dark, and I was preparing to go to bed, so I took one more quick peek out the front window. There he was, sitting pretty on the front deck. I opened the front door and invited him in, but he darted across the front yard and into the back. I realized that while the situation seemed pointless, we were also doing a bit of a dance, and Gerry was getting closer and closer to coming back to me. I brushed my teeth, and when I came back to check, Gerry was sitting on the deck right in front of the door. I had the big food bag there, so when I opened the door a crack, Gerry maneuvered himself in. He was back.

I guess he realized that life was better with us—the warmth, the food, the companionship and love. It was great to have him back—this time on his own terms, of his own free will.

Choices

My first official book signing at a well-known bookstore was an interesting learning experience. The part I liked best was the people-watching. There I was, set up with my own table filled with my cheery pink and white book while surrounded by thousands, possibly millions, of other books. I love the titles of books almost as much as the books themselves. Some of the nearby books that kept me company that day included: *The Alchemist* by Paulo Coelho, *Dear Life* by Alice Munro, *The White Princess* by Philippa Gregory, *Moment by Moment* by Jerry Braza, *To Kill a Mocking Bird* by Harper Lee, *Life After Life* by Kate Atkinson, *The Princess Bride* by William Goldman, *The Unlikely Pilgrimage* by Rachel Joyce, *The Hole in the Middle* by Kate Hilton, and *All the Light We Cannot See* by Anthony Doerr. So many books and so little time! In reality, we'll never get to all of them. Of course, not every book we'd want to read, but even the ones we'd want to, we wouldn't get to ... and we may not even be aware of them.

The people walking through the bookstore seemed sensitive to this. They were excited to be there, but appeared hurried and slightly worried. They were looking for summer reading—something to entertain them, lift their spirits, make them think, make time stand still. It's a big decision, and there's lots of distractions. All kinds of other stuff was for sale besides books, such as throw pillows, blankets, vases, candleholders, baskets, trays, teapots, tea cups and saucers, coffee mugs, cupcake decorating kits, jam, chocolate suckers, dishes, and elephant piggy banks, just to name a few.

A man strolled by my table and seemed interested in the inviting cover. He bought a copy and asked me to make it out to "Georgina." It was one of those moments that verified I'm on the right path, no matter how many books I sell at the event. Georgina is my Aunt Georgie's full name, and there are stories about Aunt Georgie and Uncle Fred in the book I was peddling. The stories bring to light the concept of living your life with no regrets, having made decisions along the way that were meaningful and essentially in tune with your life's purpose. There are also stories involving Aunt Georgie and Uncle Fred that demonstrate how coincidences can occur which are so unlikely to happen, they grab our attention and often point us, ever so gently, in the right direction.

On Following Your Dreams

For me, writing is a declaration that I am alive. In being alive, I observe. By me writing it down and you picking up the book and reading it, we have both communicated. What a glorious thing! To think that we might be able to relate to the same thing while in different spaces and places on our planet Earth is truly something to marvel at. We can learn from both ourselves and each other—and possibly even help one another through. How about that one book that changed your life or your perspective on something that in turn re-directed you in a positive way?

When I was distributing the first copy of *Stopping to Smell the Flowers* in one town, my goal was to convince at least one establishment to display it and sell it on consignment. I resisted self-conscious thoughts that this was some strange expression of the ego wanting to be heard. How horrible would that be, if it were true? There's a constant struggle among the thoughts of *Follow your dreams*, *Follow through and don't give up*, and *What are you thinking?* Those thoughts need to be balanced with the question *Is this business plan doable?* And is this even a business plan? Because successful business people would likely say no. They'd say to run for the hills, run away from myself and my idea, it will never work—it's just not sustainable. It's break-even at best. A hobby. A nice way to spend your time, but not earn a living from.

But then there is faith. There's that tapping on the shoulder that says *It can't hurt to try*. Let that notion keep you going with whatever your calling is. Balance the common-sense business plan with the heart and then let go, see what happens, and know—perhaps believe—that the journey to wherever you're going is the truth and your answer. Take baby steps while picturing the future and your goals. You don't know who you'll affect along the way, or the ripple effect you'll have on the world around you.

I've come to realize that everyone has a book in them, or a guitar ready to be picked up and strummed, or a painting in their head ready to become a reality. Even people who pursue their talents and interests struggle. Maybe they change the type of music they're playing or writing; maybe they change their painting subject or medium. It won't necessarily be easy when you finally jump in and start expressing your passion. All you need to know is that it's just necessary to start… anywhere. It's a journey, like everything else. Don't put it off.

The challenge constantly in front of us, leading to us put off our talent-related goals, is the temptation to do them "later." Once the dishes are done, once the house is tidy, once the kids have grown up. Does the house have to be clean and neat so that you have space to think? Should the reason you're here—to express yourself and help others make the world a more beautiful place—wait on dishes, tidiness, clear thinking, and calm surroundings? Perhaps start at a place where there's a balance between the two. Maybe tidy the kitchen only enough to find a coffee mug or tea cup to accompany you as you take your first few steps towards that which calls you. Don't wait to create.

Time on My Hands

"I had some time on my hands today," he said after he appeared from behind an entranceway wall to his house. The pumpkin he'd carved was oblong and lying on its side due to the sheer nature of its size. He'd carefully carved out the *Toy Story* characters on it. I regret not taking a picture, because if I had, it would have been included right here next to this sentence to show (yes, without words) the beauty and precise detail that was taken to reach the finished product.

It got me thinking about Halloween and how amazing it is that for one night of the year, most people in the neighbourhood turn all outside and inside lights on, carve a pumpkin or two, and settle in on the couch, waiting for the next trick or treat visitor to arrive. As I walked my son and daughter and her friend along the cozy neighbourhood streets, going from door to door, someone inside a home discreetly watched from behind the curtain while their partner in crime gave candy at the door. They were waiting for the right time to lower a huge, fake, black spider—somehow suspended from an eavestrough or tree—right on top of my daughter's head. Surprise!

Halloween is supposed to be eerie and gory, but I see a completely different side. I find it quite pleasant and kind and welcoming—unless my house gets egged, or the car toilet papered—but that's never happened. Let's hope it doesn't, because I like this cozy, all-inclusive party called Halloween.

Stopping to Smell the Flowers Isn't Always Easy

It's a sad thing when you've got time off and you're restless. It's a real shame, because it feels like wasted time. All the things you dreamed of doing—some fun, some not— and all you can do is sit there, stunned. I figure it's because you're slightly damaged and tired, if only from the fast pace of life. It's important to recognize and honour that.

My advice if this happens is to stop everything altogether. Take in your surroundings and just sit and observe. When I'm in this state, I have no thoughts at all, which worries me more. Usually my mental "to do" list keeps me going. I survive the busyness by doing the next most important thing. I'm unsettled by the absence of thoughts and pressing tasks. In the end, it's a control thing. Previously, your mind was busy thinking about things, such as work, the kids, or your partner's schedule compared to yours. When you finally stop and take a break, you discover that you've forgotten how to be present. Music helps with this stage, as does a bit of alcohol if it agrees with you. (Maybe Bailey's in the coffee?) Exercise and food also help, but not necessarily in that order. This is no time to diet or reduce intake. It's not a time for overeating, either. Just make sure you're fueled.

As you sit and observe, let your mind feel nothing. Watch for thoughts that arise, telling you what you need to accomplish, or thoughts that bother you, and just let them sit there. Don't judge the thoughts; let them exist, but without digging deeper into them. If lots of thoughts and ideas come up, they'll likely flood in and feel overwhelming.

Don't feel pressure to dwell on what is most important—just let those ideas sit there. Just acknowledge. Keep breathing, keep relaxing. The longer you sit, the more likely you are to focus on the one thing that hangs around in your mind more so than the others. Choose that as your task of the day and let everything else that gets in the way of completing that one focus simply fill in the blanks. Remind yourself that downtime is not a waste of time—it's just the exact opposite of busy. It helps you hit the reset button.

Sometimes stopping to smell the flowers isn't easy; however, it's necessary every now and then along the way.

A Break from the To-Do List

I decided to stop at the little park with a pretty walkway along the river. I had a huge "to do" list, none of which included stopping to smell the flowers. It was Easter weekend, and we were hosting the big dinner. I'd forgotten some key items for the dinner and was able to sneak out on my own for a little bit of quiet before the event. Something in me decided to put a halt to the busyness anyway.

I headed down to the river to check out what there was to see. The river rushed and the birds flew, and it was lovely. Someone had written "It's a girl" in pink chalk on a flat area of a tree where a large branch had previously been cut off, leaving a nice, flat surface for such messages. What a thoughtful announcement of joy; it would eventually wash off, leaving nature intact in the long run.

I enjoyed watching the fast flow of the river and decided I liked watching the water that was coming from the right as opposed to the water that was flowing to my left. I saw three mallard ducks approach; when they spotted me, they retreated smoothly back in the same direction they'd come from. They circled around again, three more times, sure of the direction they wanted to take but unsure of me standing there.

There was a sign near me that I hadn't seen before, outlining the endangered species that live there, types of fish and birds and bugs. The sign reminded us to enjoy, but carefully and with respect, just like the pink chalk temporarily shouting out a message of joy without hurting the tree.

I looked upstream again at the water that approached and my mind wandered to my childhood, when I would frequent the woods in our back yard. There was a small creek nestled in the woods, not far from the entry—no wider than the length of the sole on my rubber boot. I'd place my boot widthwise in the water in an area that had a slight decline, thereby creating my own fast-flowing waterfall. I'd watch the water caress itself over the top of my boot and continue down the little river forever. *Always remember that*, I hear in my head, my inner self giving me a gentle nod. Remember what? That nature is my refuge, where I recharge and reconnect with myself, and that's important. Cars rushed by on the road behind and slightly above me, but the river and I were immune to their activity.

I headed back to my car in the parking lot, grateful I'd decided to put everything on hold, risk a soaker, and take time out to reconnect.

The Wind

I was biking so quickly, the wind was bending my eyelashes. All the critical housework had been completed, and I now had a ten- to-twenty-minute escape to remind me of my former self. I biked faster and faster—so fast that I wondered what would happen if I fell. Imagine that— forty-year-old mother falls off bike and skins knee.

Back in the day, I would have been with my mother and father or sisters and brother, and later with my husband before we had kids. They would have known if I'd fallen. I would have been safe. But now, with the frequent tag-team approach to parenting … well, we're flying solo most of the time. What if I had fallen? What if? I didn't, though, and if I had, I would have gotten up, dusted myself off, and made my way back home to safety. Or maybe a complete stranger would have helped, just like when my son and I were biking the other day and the chain fell off his little tyke bike. I had trouble getting the chain back on, and a man on his speed walk stopped to help us. He got his hands all oily from the chain, but he didn't seem to mind. "Those are good Samaritans," I said to my son, after the man had walked on. "People who help other people they don't even know." Perhaps this man was remembering when he was in a similar situation, or maybe he was thinking of his son or daughter with their child. Certain things bring you down memory lane. I believe that whatever their reason for helping, in doing so they keep the world revolving.

The Chair in the Woods

I was driving and gazing out at the farmers' fields on either side of the highway, and off in the distance I saw a patch of woods. In the opening of the woods, just on the inside, stood a chair. Likely a thinking chair, a meditation chair, a place where you look inward and see your real self. Once you see yourself, you see others more clearly too.

I'd like to sit there.

The Funny Thing About Being a Parent

This may be a misleading title, as there's nothing funny about being a parent. What a responsibility! Funny things do happen, both to you and your children, as you learn about the world together. Funny mishaps, funny circumstances, and funny timing on things. But the "funny" I'm referring to is how, as a parent, you're too busy to notice the time go by.

The process you go through as a parent *is funny*. Take baking, for example. I enjoy baking, and it has the added benefit of producing yummy treats for the family to enjoy. A craft, if you will (and often some sort of therapy for me), with an edible end result. But the process of baking and the things I manage and go through can be quite funny.

Here's my process, which reminds me of a *Family Circle* cartoon in which you see a child's footprints outlining the meandering route taken to get to the final destination. First, I research what I fancy to bake next, looking on Pinterest, other websites, or just by visualizing my family recipe book. I make a grocery list of the items I'll need, and then decide when to make the goods. I think about which child I'll ask to help, weighing in on whom I need one-on-one time with the most, depending on what's going on in their lives. Baking is a great way to communicate with the kids while you work together; you can talk about feelings, goals, hopes, and concerns. Fast forward to the grocery store, the check-out line, the car, the driveway at the house, and into the cupboard.

The day arrives to bake, and I notice that the bag of chocolate chips has been opened by some unidentified family member needing a quick chocolate fix. No one comes forward to admit the baking ingredient crime. I let everyone know that there's still enough (but barely) chocolate chips for the recipe but warn them not to eat any more. I hide the bag of chocolate chips in a different cupboard, only to find them days later, practically obliterated.

The funny thing about being a parent is that you could easily get distracted, mad, and frustrated. In the process, you could miss the moments. You often don't get to accomplish what you set out to do, but along the way you teach (about sharing), demonstrate (how to bake and how to be patient when mistakes, like eating ingredients, happen), communicate (about how each person and their interests are important), and show love (in even considering baking something when time is tight with raising a family and having a career). There are always many options and many distractions in life. Being fully present for all the activity comes when you trust yourself.

To be fully present, whether you're a parent or not, requires knowing and practicing when to walk away and when to stay—whether you're experiencing fear, disappointment, or joy—so that you don't miss those precious moments in between.

Practice Paying It Forward

I paid it forward for the first time today. I'd been on the receiving end of a pay it forward before, and boy, what a feeling to be cared for by a stranger! A true act of love, especially without the chance to say thanks. I received a free cup of coffee in the Tim Horton's drive thru when the giver had paid for my order in advance and then driven off.

I decided to pay it forward because it happened to me again, this time at the post office. I came across someone to whom I owed money—not a lot, but it had been on my mind for months that I owed her. I pulled my money out of my wallet, excited and relieved to repay her, but she wouldn't take it! She told me to pay it forward and make someone else's day. I wound up leaving a small amount of money on the counter in front of her and told her to pay that forward too.

My next stop was the Tim Horton's drive thru (yes, frequent visits). I knew I needed to pay it forward, as it was only right, but I was slightly nervous. In this scenario, you can't predict exactly how much money you're donating, as you have no idea how much the person behind you is going to order. What if they ordered fifteen boxes of donuts and vats of transportable coffee boxes to a big event they were heading to? *Maybe I can't afford to pay it forward*, I thought. Then I slapped myself back to reality, reminding myself of the point of this whole experience! There's an element of risk in helping others—how it may affect you and also them.

I rolled up to the window and paid for my coffee. "I'd like to pay for the person's order behind me," I gulped.

She answered right away: "It's a large hot chocolate; $1.90."

I jumped for joy, because that was my kind of price for making someone's day. I paid for the goods and asked her if this kind of thing happened a lot. She assured me it did, and proceeded to tell me about the ripple effect that takes place. I hadn't thought of this before, but it's often not just the one "pay it forward" act that occurs, but a series of pay it forwards—in the drive thru line, anyway.

"It's a rolling effect," she said. "One person does it, and that causes a chain reaction from one person to the next behind them."

Of course it does. Makes total sense. Not just helping one another, but inspiring others to consider helping the next person too. We're all a part of it.

No Regrets

"I have no regrets," she said. "I've had a good life."

I'd heard those same words from another neighbour at the end of her life too, and now I was hearing them again. I was borrowing a can opener from my neighbour, and she told me that her daughter had told her to see the doctor, because something was up. I needed the can opener for my eighteen-year-old cat, who was unwell and had trouble eating soft canned food as well as hard kibble. The one food she could handle was canned salmon. We were going camping that summer and needed a can opener at the house for my sister, who'd be coming over to feed the ailing cat.

That day the doctors had poked and prodded my neighbour, and I heard those special, all-telling words again about having had a good life. I told her she could keep going and not give up, that she was only seventy-eight. She agreed in principal and said that her doctor had a plan for her, that there was hope, but she seemed to know that her journey here was coming to a close. My dear cat died on October 3, and my neighbour died on December 4 of that same year.

Every Christmas Eve in the afternoon, this neighbour of mine would knock on the front door and bring us a plate of homemade assorted baked goods, mostly squares. They were so good, it was hard to decide which one to choose first. No two were the same, so it was a big decision, especially when sharing with my husband and kids. My neighbour and I always laughed about it, because no matter what time she came over on Christmas Eve, I'd be in my housecoat with my wet hair in a towel, having been too busy during the day for a shower, and preparing to get ready for church that evening.

In the summers, we had a silent "laundry on the clothesline" competition. It wasn't ever talked about, but only felt … and likely only in my head. It went like this: if one of us got the laundry out on the line before the other one, they had grabbed the opportunity for the luxury of wind and sun-dried clothes first.

There were multiple, but short, conversations over the fence. She had a beautiful, well-tended garden, and she loved to see the kids enjoying our welcoming back yard. We had a small pool, and she knew and appreciated how much joy we got out of it. In the summers we'd see her ride her bike with admirable posture, enjoying her life. She was an inspiration to me. She'd lost her husband some thirty years previous but still found her way, still enjoyed what she did have, and didn't labour over what she didn't. Who will move in next? What will next summer be like, not seeing her on her bike or mowing the lawn? Not seeing the laundry out flapping in the wind, reminding me to get mine out? We've already experienced Christmas with no baked goods, no knock at the door to find me still in my housecoat. I suppose it's a new normal. We'll adapt, as we're genetically programmed to do. We have no other choice, really, but we'll remember her and wonder what it all means.

Keep Your Vacation with You All Year Round

"Don't get up," she said to my husband. "This is why you're here. Are you enjoying yourself so far?" The landlady had just introduced herself to us. It was summer vacation and our first time renting a cottage for our little family for longer than a weekend. "This is why you're here." I loved those words. It felt like someone understood me ... us. We did eventually get up from our comfy spot to explore the island and our surroundings. And the people we saw! The conversations we had just have to be shared.

Some people we talked to had grown up there, and they were back for a vacation. Some places they couldn't bring themselves to visit, such as school houses that had been turned into restaurants. Another day a man offered to take our family picture on the limestone rock trail that lined the lake. He was moving up there permanently, having just retired.

Conversations often and easily drifted to hobbies and crafts and callings. While waiting for our takeout dinner, we met another local who told us about the musical happenings on the island, and how my husband could join in if he wanted to. An easy conversation in the driveway with our landlady led me to tell her about the book I'd written, and I gave her a copy to look at. A few days later, her friend came over and felt she was meant to buy my book. Her father had lived on the island and was a writer as well. A visit to an art gallery later that week inspired my kids and I to create our own paintings, albeit amateur; it was still a great experience to create while on vacation.

Others who stopped to talk with us spoke of careers and raising children. Perhaps we reminded them of themselves back in the day. One woman said that you never really think the kids will grow up, but they do.

On our last evening, my son and I walked slowly home along the beach, our feet in the water, wading along. We stopped every few steps to turn and look at the amazing sunset unfolding behind us. I took a picture each time, not knowing which one would be the winner. A kayak pulled up on the shore, and the paddler got out her camera to take a picture as well. I asked her if I could get her and her kayak in my picture, as the silhouette went well with the sunset. She said that would be more than fine, and truth be told, no one had ever taken her picture in the kayak before. She gave me her email address and asked me to send the picture to her. We said goodbye and headed towards the boardwalk, which led to the road. A young lady had her camera and was headed towards the sunset to capture it on film. She asked us if the water was cold. I told her that the river fed into the lake just around the corner, and that the water was very warm there.

Just then she took off like a butterfly, distracted from our conversation by a small puddle on the beach, taking a picture of the sunset reflecting in it. I marveled at her creativity and wondered how the picture would turn out.

And then there's after the vacation. You're so tired, you can't move. You think it's from the long drive home, but then realize it's because the vacation is over. No more being in the moment (or, at least, it's harder to achieve), where the furthest ahead you look is to decide whether or not to bring your surf socks and towel with you. Once home, duty automatically starts—that old nagging in your head about all the "shoulds" that surround you. I should do the laundry; I should unpack; I should feel better.

Holidays are the ultimate experience of truly being in the moment, where thoughts of the past and summersaulting thoughts of the future are melded together in space and time that is the present.

Keep your vacation with you all through the year by asking yourself one question every day: "What can I do for myself today?" And do it. Even small things count. You'll be much better off for it.

Comfort from Books

I find comfort in all the books in the library. I love sitting near them. Once upon a time I looked at them all as competition, and they made me nervous. *How was mine different? Who was my market? How does their writing style compare with mine? Which one is better?* These questions came from the need to succeed in today's market, and the need of my ego to be sure that I should keep on writing. I needed to diffuse any doubts I had about publishing a book and promoting it—all fear-based thoughts, which look for direct results.

I see the world of publishing differently now that I'm a little bit wiser. The most important thing is if you like to write, then write. The same goes for any hobby—painting, sewing, playing a musical instrument. The ego will challenge and say things like: "Who are *you* to be doing this? *This* is what you're interested in? It sounds/looks terrible!" The sheer number of books in existence would make one think that theirs wouldn't count, or wouldn't amount to much. But when you're in the process of writing or practicing your craft, *that* is the true essence of what you should be doing. Perfect your craft later and just swim around in it now. Spend time with it and you'll be a happier, better version of yourself.

I like to look at all those books on the shelf keeping each other company. I like the notion that my book is one of them, one of the many. Some of them are on display. The display changes regularly and sets some books apart from the others—a humble but quietly proud suggestion by the librarian that it might be a good read. It might be something to keep you company, to get you through a moment in time, to give a new and different perspective. They will always exist.

I come to the library to write. I love the atmosphere. You find all walks of life here—young kids playing computer games on signed out computers, adults searching and applying for jobs on the internet, an older gentleman working on a puzzle. We're all here together on Saturday mornings. Perhaps many of us are escaping our usual environments at home and broadening our perspectives. Today, two women are working on the community puzzle, and I'm wondering what the older gentleman will think of someone else filling in the puzzle. I've never seen the women working on it before, but he's usually here like clockwork. Right on cue, he walks in and cautiously approaches the old, heavy, wooden table where the puzzle resides. He casually asks a question. They answer that they're having difficulty in one section. He jokes that some puzzle pieces on the floor might help the situation. They laugh together and pick up one of the pieces off the floor, which winds up being the solution to the problem that kept them from advancing. He waits to be invited to sit and join in, even though, unbeknownst to the women, the puzzle is his regular project. Once this occurs, they all work in silence, focusing on the task at hand.

The library is not just a place with books. It's a communal meeting place, a place to go to get away, a place to accomplish something and ultimately, to find some peace.

One Foot in Front of the Other

In between appointments for the day, I had the opportunity to stop and take in my surroundings, which just happened to be my old stomping ground while at university. Lots of people were out and about getting their daily dose of exercise and fresh air. It was a beautiful day, neither hot nor cold. The sun was shining, and it was nice to see new life as I observed the Canadian geese and their goslings. As I strolled along, I recalled walking that winding path through the endless parkway to and from the downtown core and the school. There's always that strange person, isn't there? They tend to make you question whether you made the right decision being there. There he was, sitting on a picnic table by the river, tapping to a tune coming from his big headphones, completely oblivious to his surroundings. Yet at the same time, he was aware whenever someone came near. I wondered what his story was and if he had a place to call home. I did recall those feelings of being worried about my safety, as I was often alone, traveling by foot to get from here to there. *Never mind him*, I thought, *you're here to check out your old walkway and remember.*

I walked past him as cyclists on their way to yoga class whizzed by with their yoga mats clipped to their bike carriers. Others jogged by me on the path. I saw business people on their lunch breaks walking and talking on their cell phones. One man in a business suit put on a baseball cap, and a young man with a huge skateboard was feeding the geese leftover bread. As I watched young and old around me, catching glimpses of the river rolling along and the trees gently waving in the wind, I remembered how often I frequented this path twenty years ago—not just for the trip to the city centre, with the added bonus of built in exercise, but also to escape into nature and reflect.

I passed by the bridge I used to cross over the river at a certain section, which is now closed for repair, and I remembered the hot sections on the path that aren't shaded by any trees. I approached the top of a hill as two mothers were exercising, running up the hill with small weights held above their heads. Their coach was waiting at the bottom of the hill with the strollers and their babies. I felt so proud of everybody making such an effort to exercise, be healthy, and be on the move.

It's a wonderful feeling to look back on my past and feel content. I used to look back and feel uncomfortable or slightly sad, but at that time I was still in the midst of making something out of my life that suited me. It takes time to actually become an adult. Back when I used to walk this path, I was really just putting one foot in front of the other, not sure of where I was headed or if the decisions I was making were the right ones. Now with a family, my career, and my hobbies, I know I've done my best. You only know this once you reach something and go far enough on your path in order to look back on it.

I headed down this memory trail until the clock told me I had to head back. I stopped for a bit, almost done my trek, and sat at a picnic table. A Canada goose floated backwards down the river, his head in the water trying to catch any greenery or food floating by. It made me chuckle. Other geese rode a few whitecaps that formed in certain areas of the river. I stopped and sat where the strange guy had been sitting, because that's where the shade was. When you hold still, that's when the wildlife comes out ... or rather, is observable. As I looked to my right, I saw a whole family of geese with their seven goslings roaming in the beautiful, green grass ... something I wouldn't have seen had I been walking past at my exercise pace. As my eyes wandered further to the right, I saw yet another goose family with nine goslings. In front of me, blackbirds started to pop up from the grasses, pecking at beautiful, small, purply-blue flowers as a fish jumped in the river in the background. A refreshing breeze arrived, making me never want to leave. The notion of stopping time just a little longer surrounded me.

Facing the Stuff as Time Moves On

Being a parent isn't easy … or maybe it's being human that isn't easy. We're getting ready for our annual yard sale, which sounds like fun, but it's not. What would be fun is shopping for more stuff, not getting rid of it. Or throwing a party—that would be fun. Shove everything extra into a closet, out of sight and out of mind, and just party on. So much easier. But instead, today we face what we've been up to—liking and buying one more thing and moving on to the next. My daughter starts collecting and then drops that collection and moves to another. *Repeatedly.* She thinks we need a bigger house, probably to fit in all the partial collections.

On top of that, my two kids seem completely content to move from tablet to iPod to TV screen to laptop. I gently, and as friendly and encouragingly as possible, guide them to put the electronics down and complete their homework, help me organize stuff for the yard sale, or clean their rooms. They oblige, but eventually move back to the electronic babysitters, as do I. My cell phone is my best friend. It helps me keep in touch with the outside world—a different, refreshing perspective other than my own plight.

Some say a messy house means you're spending more time doing things with your children. Gosh, I hope so, because the alternative is that we're just lazy. Let's face it, to keep up with groceries, meals, laundry, and dishes while working out of the house full time takes all you've got in the energy department to keep going.

Stephanie Malo

It turns out that what we've been up to has been diligently ignoring that time is moving on. That collections and interests get dropped. That we do change, and our stuff changes with it, and the old stuff gets left in the corner, shoved behind the door.

Yesterday we went out as a family and got groceries, a haircut for my son, and track and field shorts for my daughter. We also picked up my son's soccer jersey and made sure his new used soccer cleats fit. We do spend time together, but we need to get a bit better at facing the music and purging our belongings as life moves on. There are whole television series out there on this very subject. We don't get the channels with these shows, because we've managed to purge the satellite TV in our efforts to eliminate at least some of the distractions.

I think I'll go tear my son away from his tablet, and my daughter away from her iPod, so we can play a game of Uno on the back deck!

Blinking Lights

Why does that make me so happy? Just that simple flashing of the tail lights from the truck driver to say thanks in a "You saw me and I saw you" kind of way.

It's a similar thing when you rescue a stray animal or hold a door open at a shopping mall for the person behind you. These are all ways to recognize and honour "the other" in someone apart from yourself. You don't know the person, but somehow this moment in time has brought you together.

I smile to myself as I drive behind the trucker who took the time to thank me by blinking his taillights. The guy behind me tries to hold back his irritation at the slight slowdown I've inherently involved him in too, without intention, in my act of kindness.

We're all in this rat race together, and slowing down and recognizing others feels good.

Barbeque and Meditate

I cooked some burgers on the barbeque tonight. It's a big deal, because usually this is my husband's job. I haven't barbequed since I was a "hotdogger" during the summers of my university years. And no, it wasn't "hotdogger" as in skateboarding. It was driving and pulling a trailer to a different location each time, usually in a parking lot of a large store or mall, and setting up shop for the day. I had to hook up a propane tank to the barbeque I'd hauled there and conduct a bubble test to make sure I didn't have any leaks and wouldn't blow up myself and others around me. I sold sausages, hot dogs, and pop. All of this by myself. Even though I was in university, which sounds so official and grown up, I was really still a confused kid doing my best to follow instructions and do the right thing. It tends to be a man's job, this barbeque business, but my sales were always the highest out of all the other hotdoggers. It was a sign of what I would do in my career one day … but that, I suppose, is another story to be written on another day.

As I continued cooking the burgers, I could see the draw towards it. Lighting that barbeque, seeing the open flame, and then hearing the sizzle as you place the food on the grill reminds you of camping, but you're in the comfort of your own back yard, balcony, or wherever.

During those summers as a hotdogger, I saw many people over the course of a day drive away with their pop still on the roof of their car, having originally put it there to unlock their car while taking bites of their hotdog, obviously distracted by the more important part of their eating experience.

Stephanie Malo

When I finished barbequing and daydreaming, I noticed I'd burnt the edges of the hamburgers a bit. I promised myself to not be critical next time of my husband's barbequing. It's easy to get distracted with your thoughts while the food cooks in your own backyard oasis.

On Being Happy

I always see at least one inspiring thing on my walk. Before I head out, I always do an arm-wrestle with myself in my head. I say things to myself like, "Oh, wouldn't it be nice to just get cozy and relax on the couch? Watch TV? Just stay and get the kids to bed, or get the dishes done? There's laundry, too."

But instead, logic (or something close to it) wins out. The sun is still out, the days are getting longer, and the kids are going to be up for a while. The dishes and laundry can wait. They just multiply as soon as they're completed, anyway.

As I start my walk on the usual path, I wonder (please, please, PLEASE) if the kids will be in bed when I get home. As I ponder the chances of this, I come across the sweetest, tiniest, white dog running quickly towards me, ears flopping, legs galloping. At first I wonder if she intends to nip my ankles. Maybe she's defending her turf. But I soon realize she's just happy to have found me. She reaches me and, with the sweetest look on her face, bends her head in such a way as to invite a friendly scratch on the jaw and behind the ear. If she could speak, she'd say, "Oh my *goodness*! I'm getting a massage! Life is so good!" As I continue on my way, I see the owner of this sweet dog at the last minute in his driveway, and we talk about how great it would be if everyone was that happy and joyful every day.

Towards the end of my walk, I catch a glimpse of a father and son sitting in chairs at the front of their house. They're tucked away in a corner by the front door, a blanket covering their legs. The dad is quietly reading to his son; it sounds like a novel about spies and secret agents. The child listens in wonder as the sun gently says goodnight on the horizon.

I silently hope that the kids are still up when I get home so that I can read them each a story before they sleep.

Purpose

"I wake up every morning and think to myself, *How can I make someone happy today?*" he said.

Earlier, we'd heard a knock at the boardroom window. All I could see from where I was were a pair of arms waving at the window, motioning to my co-worker. I repositioned myself to see better, and saw him tell her to smile while she worked. Just the notion of someone asking her this made us both laugh. The man was a community member at a senior's centre where we were working for the day.

We went on completing our work, and some twenty minutes later, there was a knock at the boardroom door. The same man re-appeared, bearing gifts. He brought my co-worker a solar powered flower that rocked back and forth, and I received chocolates. He explained to us that he likes to make people happy each day.

"That's great," I said, and we talked about how making others happy really is a gift to ourselves, because it makes the giver feel great.

When our work was finished that day, we held a summary meeting with our co-workers. The happy-looking, red and green flower watched while rocking back and forth in the centre of the table. We also shared purple, individually wrapped, heart-shaped chocolates, trying hard to remember not to take life so seriously.

The Library

I really can't say enough about the library. I mean, *really*.

First off, it's meticulously kept. Everything's in order amidst the chaos of life outside. Just go in there and breathe that in. Where is it? Here. What is it? This. Why? When? How? All answered for you. Sure, you can search for all these answers on the internet, but you can't visually see the order. You get suggestions, which almost makes you think you need to do some organizing. The library—already organized.

The amount of resources available amazes me too. From newspapers to magazines to water testing kits. What's that? Pick up your water testing kit and bring it back to the library, because someone regularly comes to pick it up and get it tested for you. Need to rent a space to hold a book club or meditation group, writing group or art club? You bet! Reasonable rates and flexible schedules. Absolute bliss.

Want to work on a puzzle? It's there, and it's a community event. No need to stress over storage of the puzzle while it's being worked on. Share the work with no commitment on your part.

Order a book to borrow from a completely different library system in another city and have everyone work on your behalf to let you know that it's in and when it's due back.

Not to mention e-books and movies and children's programs.

My friend told me that at the library where she grew up, they now loan fishing poles. Fishing poles from the library. Give fishing a try

Stephanie Malo

without spending a dime. Yes, please. Thank you, library. Thank you, modern society. I think I'll give it a try.

Retracing Your Roots

I sat at the creek's edge amongst tiny yellow flowers, grand tall trees, butterflies and birds soaring and fluttering. This was the spot, I was sure of it, which would help the story that follows come out.

If I looked either left or right, I could see the winding creek's path through the glorious wild flowers and forest. The library is my usual go-to place for writing, but it wouldn't suffice today. The library often inspires me, just being near all those books, but for today's story I needed to feel the ground. I had a story to write that would take a lot of courage to figure out the words. The story came from an opportunity I had, once again while traveling, to stop and smell the flowers.

I had a fair chunk of time before my appointment, as I'd left early to beat the traffic for this longer-than-usual trip. I happened to be in the town where my grandparents used to live, where we'd visit them when I was a young kid. I decided to take advantage of this opportunity and drive to where they used to live. I sat in my car in front of the house, remembering. Some trees on the front lawn were gone, but otherwise the place looked the same as I remembered it. But sitting there in my car wasn't enough. Like a moth to the light, I was drawn to the door. I made my way down that familiar driveway, which I hadn't walked on in some thirty years, and rang the doorbell.

What will I say if someone answers? I heard my brain ask myself. *I suppose I'll just say hello and tell the strangers that my grandparents used to live there. Maybe they'll invite me in for tea, let me look around.*

It's probably for the best that no one was home. I might have been a frightening mess of tears and emotion—not a good way to be before my appointment, which was the reason I was in this town in the first place. As I stood there waiting for someone to answer, I discretely peeked through the window to see that all was the same as I remembered, just with modern furniture.

As I turned away and headed back towards the driveway, I took a picture of the back yard in which we spent so much time when we visited. It looked exactly the same as the snapshot of it in my head after all these years—the fire pit, the gardens, the trees lining the back of the yard. My grandpa was a gardener, both vegetables and flowers. Stories of his love of gardening inspired me to try a dahlia garden years ago with much success. Even though I had to painstakingly take the bulbs out of the ground each fall in preparation for the winter and plant them again in the spring each year, it always made me think of him. If Grandpa could do it, so could I. The dahlia gardening brought me much joy.

I made my way back to my car and sat down. I wondered what I would have looked like to anyone else that knew me, to be there knocking on the door of the past and asking to be let in—just one more conversation, just one more chance, one more possibility to connect.

Would you believe that on my way home after my appointment, I stopped by the home where I grew up? Very likely too much for one day, but I was determined. We often don't schedule when or how we're going to stop and smell the flowers. My parents had moved about two years earlier to be closer to their kids and grandkids. They'd lived in this house for over forty years. Did I ring the doorbell here too? You bet I did. Ringing the doorbell at both my parents' and my grandparents' houses gave me a sort of grand out-of-body experience. Not something I'd want to experience on a regular basis, but neat, just the same.

No one answered here, either; all probably at work. And what would I have said, anyway? I used to live here? So? Then what? I noticed that the place looked well-kept and well loved, so I decided right there and then to release the past into the unknown and just know that I am safe no matter where I am, as long as my loved ones are around me. Once this was decided, I headed home in their direction.

As I drove, I realized that because of the busyness of daily life—filled with children, meals, and laundry—the dahlia planting had been forgotten. Not a priority. It had been years since my beautiful dahlia garden had been in bloom. I'd recently discovered some bulbs in the basement where I'd tucked them years ago. Right then and there I decided that as soon as I got home, I would plant them.

If you ever have a chance to visit the past, do so. Don't stay long, just take a glimpse. Just enough to remind you. It can be very grounding, this reminder of where you come from, where you are now, and where you want to be in the future.

Life Coming to a Halt

I remember hearing the ear-piercing, screeching sound of a train coming to a halt in the darkness of the night. It was eerie and dragged on, desperately longing and groaning for stillness. I was hearing it from far away, but the night was so still, you could hear every detail of its efforts to slow down. When it finally did, it felt like the universe had come to a stop. Finally, silence. Deafening silence. The tick, tick, tick of the clock, and then the sound of the sirens wailing down the road. I later found out that the train had tried to stop because there was a car on the tracks. The driver had died, likely a suicide. He was a father, a husband. He was troubled by money and making ends meet. He had given up.

During the time of silence between the end of the screeching train and the sound of the sirens, I had some thoughts. I'd been standing in my kitchen grabbing a quick bite to eat in the middle of the night, as a bit of anxiety had gotten me up. I thought about people I knew who were struggling, about how my daughter is growing up, and specifically how she no longer wanted a kiss or hug goodnight. I thought about my parents aging. Sometimes stopping to smell the flowers means seeing the change, seeing how life is different, how it changes, how it can slip through your fingers as you dutifully lead it in the best way you can.

It's a confusing and ever-changing world, never leaving you thinking about the same thing twice. It would be easy to let these things get you down, but then there are the other things—the dates with my husband and reconnecting after the early years of child rearing;

baking with my son, who's still interested in being with his mom and using the new, colourful Charlie Brown measuring cups; hot tub talks with my sister; the listening ear of a friend; sitting in a coffee shop with my mom. These are stolen, precious moments in between the shocking bits. The glue that holds us together. The sounds in between the good and the bad in life.

The change that seems negative also brings change that is positive. To get you through the negative, listen to music in your car so loudly that it hurts your ears. Picture shopping for your favourite clothes in your favourite store. See the colour of a flower—really see it. Imagine each thought as a cloud, one by one whisking along. It's real, but it can't touch you as it moves along on its way. Picture happy vacation places you've been to, including destinations you've yet to visit.

Never give up. You will get through this.

Teaching Fear by Accident

How easy it would be to only teach our kids about fear, I thought as I stared at my son in response to his question. I could teach him about the "what ifs" instead of the "why nots." He was nine years old and asking me if he could go on a trip to a destination an hour and a half away with his friend and his friend's parents. I thought of all the ways he could encounter danger, including but not limited to: driving on the highway, getting lost in the big city, staying in a hotel, and playing dangerously in the pool.

"Of course you can go," I answered, trying to sound normal, to feel good about the decision, to trust.

There's the upside of the things learned while doing, or allowing someone you love to do, that which frightens you. The experiences can be so powerful, they shape us. And if they're not experienced at all, if fear wins, then it's an experience lost. It's fearful to realize, upon examination, that you could miss an opportunity for growth because of fear. The answer, I believe, between doing and not doing lies somewhere down the middle of the two paths. Know your risks, but don't let them stop you. Be knowledgeable and then free yourself to experience.

How will we ever manage to let go once he leaves home for good? I wondered. Of course, it will be done in baby steps, and we will have taught him the best we could. We should be proud of ourselves, because we will have taught him, within reason, not to be afraid.

The Cottage

We never really own the land. We pay to borrow it for a while. The land will be there for the next people and the next.

I often think of the land on which my parents' cottage was built. It started out as two separate postage-stamp sized lots with already-existing rickety cottages on each.

I remember lying in the tall grasses behind the cottage, feeling at one with the land. No one knew I was there with the foliage blowing in the breeze covering up my tracks, and my body lying within it. It was thinking time for me. Another thinking place was down at the water's edge, where I would lie on small-to-medium-sized rocks that had been warmed by the sun. It was therapeutic, I'm sure of that. I would wriggle my way to a comfortable position in order to lie there for a good half hour while the sun's energy soaked into my body and melted my worries away.

When we first drove up to the lot before my parents bought it, I didn't bother to look up from my studying to even glance out the window. I was busy preparing for my final exams and didn't think that this would be the place they were looking for. I didn't give it a second thought. Little did I know that it would be the place where I'd see the constellations the clearest I've ever seen them, the place where I'd go to recharge and be reminded that everything will be okay, the place I'd one day have to say goodbye to.

Never did I dream I'd start the process of saying goodbye to my parents. I see them age, and there's nothing I can do about it. I can only be there for them and with them, be present. Whereas the land will be there for the next and the next people, the body has a time limit. It's the way it is. Nothing about it is easy. The saving grace in saying goodbye to the land, goodbye to the body, is that the memories are not a thing of the past; they come with us, along our path, as long or short as our path may be. All the memories and moments are important puzzle pieces in our individual journeys, telling us who we are, what's important to us, and how we need to lead our own lives.

Content

I don't have a need to collect rocks today, to look at their intricacies and decide if they're worthy to keep or not.

I look at the high waves I just swam in with my children. My husband eventually joins us, having had enough rest on the beach that his shivers from tiredness have faded and his energy has returned.

I see what I have. I don't see what I don't have. I see what's in front of me, and it's good. I'm at peace, if only for these few clear moments.

I usually look for sparkle in the rocks, or a deep colour, knowing full well they won't look the same once we're home and they're dry. A futile, but enjoyable attempt to capture the day's moments.

On Letting Go

The so-called sandwich generation simultaneously and ever so slowly releases control of their kids as they grow up while also letting go of the notion that their own parents can protect or help them in any way. It's like the art and sport of synchronized skating, slowly stepping away from parenting their children as they grow and evolve while inching towards parenting their parents. Both the children and the elderly want and need their independence, and our job, as now parent to both, is to guide. This process can be painful, because it's not a straight line. Like skating, you glide from one direction to the next, this way then that, and try to average a straight line to your goal. Some days you're over so far on one side or the other, it feels like progress may be impossible. It's the art of letting go while reeling in closer, of respecting each other's boundaries, with love being the constant current running beneath it like a river. Both the kids and the aging parents need you, but both are moving towards leaving you. One day, if all goes according to plan, the kids won't live with you. And one day your parents will no longer be present ... in this world, at least. This will repeat over and over, as it did for our ancestors and their ancestors before that.

How do we get through this? One tactic is to acknowledge the good you see in those whom you parent. That's a surefire way to garner respect and to foster a joy-filled relationship. Tell them what they do well. Let them know you see their true essence. It's also equally important to look after yourself as you facilitate this process of letting go. Remember the things you like to do and do them. Carve out time for yourself. The more people need you, the more they need you to be ready to help. The only way to help well is to be as rested and re-charged as possible. Recharging comes from doing the things you like. You are important as this epicentre of inevitable change.

Light in the Darkness

The minister was ringing the bell this time, pulling on the long, thick cord to call the people. Normally the church caretaker tends to the rope. That's one of the benefits of being almost late—you get to see these things that you normally wouldn't. The minister asked my son if he'd like to try. He turned down the opportunity, but now I regret not asking if I could instead. That's one of the downfalls of always rushing to the next moment.

What is it that draws me to this particular service each year? I wonder to myself. This is the Maundy Thursday service, the day before Good Friday, in which members of the congregation offer to have their feet washed by the minister, an act of humbleness on the part of both the receiver and the giver, the reminder that we are all the same in a basic, spiritual way.

This is also the service in which the altar is stripped of all its décor—the tapestries, the table cloths, and the ornaments glistening in the church light. The golden cross at the altar is covered by a sheer black cloth. The lights are dimmed, almost to the point of darkness. The minister kneels at the altar in so much darkness, you could almost imagine she's not even there. I strain my eyes and see that she is still there, just motionless.

The church lights continue to dim, slowly in one area of the church and then the next, until the entire building becomes darker. I notice that the stained-glass windows get brighter and more colourful in contrast, perhaps picking up light from outside.

Stephanie Malo

Then I get it, the reason why I'm drawn to this somewhat somber service. It's a reflection inward. You have to experience the darkness to see the light. You have to strip away all the armour and shiny coverings to see the true light of who you are, your deepest self, your true self. Your soul.

Take Time Out

I'd been feeling angry and unsatisfied with the world around me and the people in it. When one makes a regular practice of focusing on the positives—what's working and what one is grateful for—it can be difficult to recognize when to take a time out. I was frustrated with people's reactions, questions, and concerns. I understood why they had those concerns and reactions, but I was numbed by it, not knowing where to turn. When you feel like this, it's important to talk to a friend or caring family member, as I did. They suggested that I needed a day off work and away from the family to be on my own. My first reaction was to insist that I was fine. I wasn't sick, so why use up holiday or sick time? The more I thought about it, the more I was drawn to the notion of time by myself, which I never had anymore … at least when at home.

When I took time alone at home, I had to fight the urge to "get things done." It felt like stolen time to get ahead of the chores, and an opportunity not to be missed. I resisted laundry, groceries, and dishes. I started with yoga while playing a meditation podcast and then moved to tackle the two drawers in my bedside table that hadn't been purged (or even viewed) for thirteen years' worth of accumulation.

The bottom drawer went well. I discovered fairly standard items: that book, those electronics cords, essential oil samples, a string of mini lights, and craft idea books for Christmas and Easter. I flipped that one right open to one craft we did years ago—success!

But the top drawer, the second purging … oh. I found poems my mom had written long before Parkinson's disease robbed her of absolutely all hobbies and sense of independence. I found notes I'd made on achieving my goals from my first book. Still the same goals now, still the same fears. Not much has changed except the passing of time, as my mother's poems point out. The first poems I included in *Stopping to Smell the Flowers: Extraordinary Observations on Everyday Life* were about her grandchildren, the joy they brought, and their spirits, which she could feel. The poems I found in this drawer were about the empty nest and the feeling of pride in her children, but also of loss and how life moves on.

I found a baby-raising techniques pamphlet, baby car seat manuals, cell phone plans from three phones ago, perfume so old it smelled like the past and how I used to think—no longer current. I found a tooth chart pointing out when teeth come in and when they fall out. Constant change measured within the realm of normalcy and what to expect. I also found a story, handwritten, that I had forgotten I'd written, about my daughter coming of age.

Evolving

There she was, just sitting there eating her banana. "We learned about fog, smog, and dew today, Mom," she said as she stared off into the back yard, not really looking at anything in particular.

Where did she come from? I thought. Her long, lanky legs draped comfortably over the back-deck furniture, her bangs easily falling to the side of her freckled face. Something was different; she'd evolved again. There was a palpable change. Is this not a miracle, that we can do this as humans (and animals)? Reproduce and raise our youth, perhaps to go farther than we have, maybe into unknown territory, carrying on after we're gone? What a footprint we all make on the world, each day with the opportunity to do good, to lead the way to be kind to each other.

> *This is the end of my spinning a web,*
> *the fruit has been caught and matured and fed.*
> *Now to gently dismantle the thread,*
> *to weave new beginnings*
> *of a gentler notion.*
> *Till the end of purpose and promotion.*
>
> ~ Vicki Bergmann

The Jog of My Life

I was finally sitting down and eating a big piece of apple pie, relaxing on the back deck and taking in the moment. I was surprised that this piece of pie still existed and that no one had gotten to it first. Mid-bite, my daughter came up to me and suggested going for a jog together. She just stood there, casually waiting for my response, while I tried not to outwardly show the panic that had set in. We silently stared at each other as the side of me that considered going, that wanted to spend more time with her and understand her world better, wrestled with the part of me that didn't feel like going. I couldn't believe that I was currently eating pie, how my real goal was inaction, and how jogging was such a stark contrast to what I wanted in that moment.

"Of course I'll go." Of course. I put the pie down. It suddenly didn't taste as good. I wasn't so hungry. It had been more of a comfort thing that I was going for. I had the opportunity to jog with my daughter, who, since she started the tween stage, just didn't interact as much as she used to. I changed into my jogging attire (it had been years), and we met in the driveway to stretch.

We actually jogged together for approximately 6.5 seconds. Her long legs and long-distance endurance were no match for my walk-jog-walk style. (I think we should name this *wog*.) *Oh well*, I thought, *we're still doing something together. Just because she's up ahead of me, that's no big deal.* And then she turned the corner and was no longer visible.

I was literally jogging alone. *How funny*, I thought. I'd put pie down to do something with my daughter, and I was alone. It started to get dark. I tried to guess her route, tried to read her mind, but each time I turned a corner hoping to see her up ahead, I didn't. To prevent panic, I visualized myself bringing up the rear, believing that she was just up ahead of me, and I was the mother goose making sure that all returned home. I remembered everything I'd taught her about the world and safety and independence. I trusted she was alright.

When I finally got home, she was waiting on the front deck for me, smiling.

"What took you so long, Mom? I've been home for ten minutes."

My goal was reached. The goal to bring her into this world to succeed at the small and the big things. She will be alright. And so will I.

The Art of Being Present

Everyone is out early, walking the boardwalk along the beautiful sand beach. Many are older, making the most of the day before the bones become achy.

I make my way into town and buy a postcard and coffee and settle in for a few solitary moments. The postcard is for my ninety-five-year-old aunt. I want to let her know that my mom received her birthday gift and that it was treasured, and so is she. I write it with a pencil, as it's all I can find, but I'm happy to have limited resources. My hand goes carpal tunnel numb from all the canoeing and kayaking we've done so far, so I hang it down at my side periodically to regain feeling in it.

I discover that it costs $1 plus tax to mail the postcard. I instantly feel old, but in a good way, remembering when stamps were $0.38.

People say hi here. They stop and talk to you and genuinely seem interested. Is it because we're on an island? Maybe it's a feeling that we all have something in common, and we can ask each other what part of the island we're from, as opposed to being on a greater expanse of land where we may assume we have less in common.

Later in the day we paint by the river's edge. The place we have rented has a lake and a river, and we call ourselves lucky because of it. To get to our spot, we have to walk along a narrow path through a dense forest. As we paint, my teenage daughter looks younger and less concerned about being a teenager, and she lets her creativity flow.

My son jumps into the deeper part of the river, the only place deep enough to truly swim freely, and lets his anxieties over an upcoming new school year and the notion of growing up go for a while.

I can't help but notice how unwinding feels—like layers and layers peeling off, slowly but surely. Deeper and deeper, closer to our true selves. It's an uncomfortable, painful process, almost a mind game between your ears, fighting your heart and your soul. *Don't let go, don't let in*, says your ego. *Protect yourself from who you truly are. Surely it can't be safe to be you, to be the kid you were but now as an adult. There are bills due, the responsibility of raising your kids, caring for your aging parents. Don't let go of control. What will happen if you follow your dreams?* What *could* possibly happen?

As I continue to observe my layers peel, I notice how automatic it was for my brain to be so far into the future and not fully present in each moment. I experience constant thoughts of "woulds" and "shoulds" and "coulds."

It isn't until the end of vacation—after swimming, reading, shopping, and playing tennis (and then more swimming and shopping) that I start to observe my thoughts and surroundings. My thoughts are more pleasant and less anxious when I'm not getting too far ahead of myself. Worry still comes, but without the emotion and fear. I start to see things for what they are in the present moment. It seems as if no matter what, we will figure it out, we will march on, and we will see ourselves through.

Spread Your Wings

The weather had finally turned from cold, grey, damp, and sharply dismal to sunshine and a light breeze. I could hear the birds chirping. We walked along the river's edge; the water came right to the edge of the grass walkway we were meandering along. The kids chirped their own rhetoric back and forth, saying things like "Don't walk too close to me" and "Can I borrow your cell phone to take another picture?" They laughed at me as I mixed up my words. I was tired to the point of self-induced anxiety, and I'd come to the river with my entourage on this first beautiful day of the year to seek solace and to heal. More bantering over the use of my cell phone ensued, which sent my son and I into a squabble. Soon all four of us spiraled into argumentative frustration with each other. The tree roots on a hillside acted as nature's stairs, so I decided we'd climb them to the trestle. Maybe looking out over the water would bring me the serenity I was looking for.

It was a beautiful view from way up high, the river taking a beautiful, curved swirl around grassy farmland and continuing far off into the distance. The kids noticed someone had dropped an old television that had landed face first in a shallow part of the river. *How long will that take to decompose?* I wondered. Then I pictured someone doing river clean up and allowing it to decompose elsewhere. As we walked along the trestle, I noticed my son hanging back, still miffed that I didn't let him take one more picture with my phone. The farther away I got from him, the more aware I became of how high up I was. I started to feel dizzy. We decided to split up for a bit; my husband would bring the kids for a visit with their grandparents who lived close to our current river location.

I felt a pang of guilt that it was obvious to everyone that I needed to be alone. Alone means *not with*. It's difficult to let your loved ones know you need a break. From them? Not really, but sort of. I've somehow been assigned the role of bringer of happiness for others, and the only way to successfully do that is to recharge and get the happiness for myself first. They drove to the grandparents' house, and I slowly walked my way back to them along the river's edge.

My destination was the waterfall, my last attempt of the day to soothe my soul. I sat on a large limestone rock and stared at the waterfall. I could see the water spill over the entire width of the river from up close. It hit the spot and did the trick for me. It was as if I'd given the water permission to take my continuous, anxious thoughts over the lip of the waterfall and down and away from me. At the same time, it made me aware of exactly *how many* thoughts were actually occurring at a rapid rate and on a regular basis … as rapid as the rush of the springtime water surge. I let all the thoughts, even though important, become meaningless. In doing so, I found some truth, peace, and reassurance of my self-ness, that it's all going to be okay.

Just then, I saw two mallard ducks approaching the waterfall. They'd glided in along the river but were now in close proximity to some real danger. A woman stood beside me with her professional camera to take a picture of the ducks on the river. I'd seen her on the trestle earlier taking pictures. Just as the female duck reached the edge of the waterfall, my eyes bugged out. I wondered if she was going to plummet over the falls. She spread her wings at the last moment and became airborne, making a swoop up that was the inverse motion of the shape of the water traveling down. The photographer, having intended to take a picture of ducks on a river, wound up capturing that moment when she spread her wings and soared.

Right Where We're Supposed to Be

There we were, right in the middle of a group of about thirty university students. Their average age was twenty-one, and ours forty-six. We tried to lie low, but our creaky bones complained loudly as we tried to sit still on a hardwood floor. Our slightly-grey hair and ever so slightly weathered faces also gave us away. It was all in the name of music, and no one seemed to mind us in their midst.

We'd met one of three musical bands performing that night while on summer holidays, and this was our chance to hear them play again. I'd kind of invited ourselves to their next gig near us, in some sort of desperate move to hear their unique music that seemed to take me away to another place, but also one that was right here.

The first two acts were single performers. One of the first numbers was a song the young man wrote while walking along the sidewalk in his neighbourhood. As he started to sing about the simple subject of walking, I remembered doing the same when I was at university a few decades ago. During one walk on a drizzly, fresh spring night I experienced a moment of clarity. Each step I took along the sidewalk gave me a clearer feeling, or idea, which grew stronger with each step. I had a growing clarity that I was right where I was supposed to be. It was even more powerful than words, or time, or connection. Music makes you do those things, like drift off to another place you once inhabited. That's one of the many things I like about it.

So there we were, all cramped in together and enjoying the sweet sounds and being prompted by the performer to sing along to the chorus of his song: "Right where I'm supposed to be." We sounded great together. Age or life circumstance dissolved into a single knowing of what it is to be alive.

Talk to Me, Honey Bee

Stories about coincidences are hard ones to write. In-person is much better, because you can wave your arms, bug your eyes out, and stress certain words while telling the listener about how magical your experience was, how statistically unlikely it was to happen, and how you feel like you got a message from the universe. Pen and paper force you to really hone in on and communicate what was so special.

My latest coincidence happened around a bee, as in a honey bee. The mentioning of bees was coming at me with such frequency, it was like electrical shocks. What it told me was to pay attention, without a doubt.

The first bee occasion originated from me. We had potential new business come up at work, which is always a good thing. I wanted to thank someone who had come out of retirement temporarily to help us with the sale. I thought of getting her a bee charm on a key chain from a wonderful shop I'd recently discovered. The shop is full of charms for charm bracelets or create-your-own necklaces—a unique place to get a gift that says thanks. Over the last year I'd slowly built my own charm bracelet, with each charm representing a different talisman, reminder, or source of strength for what my life was requiring at the time. It's a bit of a road trip to get to this shop, so I was looking forward to making the trip. I thought I'd add a bee to my charm bracelet too, as the person I was buying it for had once told me a story about bees. The fact that bees can actually fly with their large body and small wings defies physics. I love this. Anything can happen.

In the meantime, I made regular trips to the library, my favourite place to be and do my writing. I always start the writing process by wandering through the library, looking at all the titles, and daydreaming about what words and thoughts the books may contain. I picture the author getting the idea for it and actually writing it. I discovered a new section with selected books on display, reading suggestions from the librarian. From this display, I wound up reading a record number of books over the course of a few months. The suggestion that a good reader makes a good writer always haunts me, so I was really proud of myself for accomplishing this.

One of the books I read stopped me in my tracks. It was as if I was meant to read it. It wound up changing my thoughts on a difficult situation in my life. I was at a crossroads of sorts, and it helped me step over to something new. Part of the book concerned a person who felt a calling to write their first novel. They knew little about the novel, but they knew it would be about bees. The author-to-be felt strange about her idea, not really trusting herself. While looking at a monument that held meaning for her, she noticed a bee randomly sitting on her shoulder. The bee stayed there for quite a while, giving her a sign and the confidence to write the book. At the same time that I finished reading this book, I went to hear my husband's band perform. Their final song was a newly-written one they'd never performed, called "Honeybee."

The next day I told my son about the bee references. He liked my story with the three bee coincidences. When I asked him to start packing his lunch for school, he said that he had to record the rest of the movie he was watching—*The Bee Movie*. We stared at each other and bugged our eyes out, astonished together. Now my son was part of these coincidences.

I experienced more bee coincidences than this, some smaller and not as easy to explain. Perhaps they were happening so frequently, they became part of my regular existence. I finally found my way to my wonderful charm lady's shop to get the bee charm for the person who'd helped me out. We had a wonderful conversation about the bee. She asked me if the bee charm I was purchasing symbolized someone's passing. I said no, that it symbolized my writing and the need to believe in it and keep going. We discussed how the world around us has an energy that is so close, just below the surface, it's readily available for anyone who wants to tap into it. This strong energy is love, and it communicates. It's like a light that's too bright to look into, like water that's so clear with a current so strong, there's no need for whitecaps. It is true peace. The modern world isn't set up for talking about it or tuning to it. Coincidences can be one form of communication from this current of love-filled energy, just to remind us of it.

As we said goodbye, this charmed lady and me, I noticed she had a thank you card hanging on the wall behind her—with drawings of bees on it.

May you find your calling and have the bravery to follow your heart.

Sure, I'll Go

My son had come to church with me for the Maundy Thursday service. He was up for going, not knowing what the service was about, and having to leave the house right away after supper with the rain pouring down and the wind whipping in the dark.

We got there just as the service started. We took off our rain-soaked coats and settled in. This was the service about betrayal, about death and then rebirth. At one point in the service, the minister washes some of the congregation's feet, symbolic of the message of humility and that we're all the same, no one better or superior than another.

The grand and solemn finale is the stripping of the altar. Twelve ladies wearing white gloves, likely representing the twelve disciples and, as I like to think, the twelve months of the year, slowly, methodically, and gracefully take items from the altar. The minister then places a sheer black cloth over the cross at the altar. The congregation understands that they're to leave in silence now that the church service is over. One by one the interior lights of the church are turned off. Slowly people get up, put their jackets on, and leave the church in quiet contemplation. My son and I continue to sit, enthralled with the silence and the progressive darkness. We both notice that as it gets darker, the large, stained-glass windows high above the altar glow even more without any light in the church. An outdoor spotlight lights them up, and wisps of moisture vapor rising from a heating exhaust makes the windows look spiritual, magical, and enlightening. I glance over at my eight-year-old son and can just make out his silhouette in the darkness, hands together, eyes closed in prayer.

Most are gone from the church now, but my son and I remain. We can see that the minister is kneeling at the altar, silently in prayer, inconspicuously off to the side, holding so still you can hardly tell she's there.

We eventually leave, and as we walk back to the car, my son says he thinks that experience was awesome. I ask him what he prayed about, and he says that he prayed with thanks that he has a house to live in, good parents, and that he's safe. A real prayer of appreciation. The Maundy Thursday service is my most favourite of them all. Christmas is exciting, Easter Sunday so joyful, but Thursday is reflective. It's humble and carries the important message that we're all on the same journey, and that's at the heart of it all.

Blessings Raining Down

I listen to the sounds, part of my daily meditation practice to be fully present, if even just for a few quality moments. I hear the creak of trees, the gentle roar of the wind, the click of the leaves as they fall from the tree, and the sound of the kids playing along the water's edge farther down the river. Most of the leaves wind up in the river and gently float to who knows where. Some of the leaves helicopter down, others zig zag down, down, down, and others skydive. There's a continuous flow of these leaves down the river, happy to have hitched a ride to somewhere. As I watch them go by, my thoughts go with them, one by one, peeling away the layers of everyday thoughts. I realize that, for me, the past year has held many losses, most in the form of dramatic change, some in the form of the actual death of friends.

My husband and I decide to say a prayer and allow the leaves to take our sorrow away. As we pray, a sudden gush of wind pushes hard, and leaves come raining down—so much so that you can hardly see the river from the leaves.

I'm sure we both thought, sitting together by the river on that autumn day, that no matter how hard the road, no matter how sad or challenging, joy is also there raining down on us, blessing us, hearing us, seeing us.

Imprints

After we've died, I wonder if we've changed the world a little because of our presence, because of who we were and who we affected. We may have touched the lives of people we don't even know, such as someone behind us in line at the grocery store. Perhaps it was a kind word given to someone that didn't just make them feel better but actually shifted the course of humankind. How could it be that powerful? Shift one person, who shifts another, who shifts another in turn, and your impact is immeasurable. These acts, which we're all capable of, aren't premeditated or calculated and don't take much effort at all. At the heart of these comments, acts, and thoughts is love. What is love? Maybe you're thinking that you don't love strangers, as you don't even know them. But it's a simple kind of love, one in which the core message is this: *We are all one and the same.* If you truly feel this, you begin to treat others as you would like to be treated. If we all adopted this notion, the world would be a different and better place. The opposite concept is that we're all in competition, and we don't want to share.

I also wonder if this shift in the universe when someone dies has an equal and opposite effect as when someone is born. A new baby causes a shift in people, habits, beliefs, and love. This shift is easier to picture than when someone dies, and that's only natural. Birth is an obvious gain—a new person, a new life that we can see, assist, affect, and actively love. Death, however, holds its seemingly insurmountable loss, making it hard to see the beauty. I wonder if the world is actually growing and moving with each death as well as each birth.

The Baby Shower

This time the shower was for my sister-in-law. I hate to say it, but the lead up to the shower felt different than that of my sister's baby showers. One reason is probably because I'd aged since the last baby shower. I'd seen more of life in general, which inevitably changes you. The biggest reason, though, was that this baby-to-be was part of my brother. My brother was born when I was twelve years old, so I was mature enough to be responsible for him—change his diapers, babysit him when my parents went out, and teach him to dance around the coffee table. When he was five years old, he asked me why I was leaving home to go to university. I had trouble explaining to a five-year-old why anyone would ever want to leave. He was a big focus of my life and a very special person.

I suppose this baby shower gave me a *little* taste of what it might be like to be a mom to a son who is going to be a father. I felt vulnerable. Seeing a few items in the baby section of a popular store made me at once realize that 1) If my brother is going to have a baby, then I'm getting older, and 2) I won't be having any more kids. (Not having more kids had already been a conscious decision, but this made it more real.) I could see exactly how fast parenthood goes by before your eyes.

The baby shower turned out to be fun. The mom-to-be's sister graciously organized the whole thing, and I'd never had so much fun playing shower games. I felt that I got to know my sister-in-law's family even more than before. This baby business is tricky—it makes you realize your own place in the world, and at the same time that you have to make room for others.

I'd made the cake for the shower. When I spoke to my sister-in-law's aunt, I asked her if she was the one who'd made my sister-in-law's first birthday cake, which I'd heard about. She said yes, that was her, and that she'd hoped to make the shower cake for today's event too, but had found out that I was doing it.

Oh no, I thought. I couldn't believe I'd taken her spot by accident. It put all my vulnerable feelings in place. I then realized that everybody was vulnerable as we waited to see what this new baby would bring to us and the world. Everybody's children grow fast, so everybody is challenged to adapt as life changes right before our very eyes, each and every day, week, and year.

As we were about to leave the shower, the aunt said, "You did a good job." Together we took the remainder of the cake off the tray and packaged up my belongings to take home. It was my nod from the universe telling me that it will all turn out alright. A reminder to just keep putting one foot in front of the other. Change is inevitable, but so is our ability to change with it.

The Sounds of Silence

I was certain I could hear the snow melt. It wasn't that drip, drip, drip sound you're likely imagining. I'm not sure exactly *what* I was hearing, but I swear it was crackling and popping, like the sound those popping candies make as they dissolve in your mouth. A time-release camera would have revealed that the snow was melting under my watchful eye, but all I could see for certain was a tiny bug crawling along. As I watched it, I realized I hadn't seen one of those in over five months. Imagine it coming out of its hiding place after all that protected time!

The kids and I had gone for a walk in the nearby woods. The sun was shining and the water in the creek had begun to move, the ice having just melted. I called the kids back to me from the creek where they were wading to listen to the snow melting.

With a child on either side of me, we stood there, saying nothing. The first thing we heard was the ding of my cell phone—my husband letting me know that he was headed home from his appointment. In a way, he was there with us as we listened. We not only heard faint crackles and pops from the snow dissolving, but also a moaning, creaking sound from the trees as the snow started its melting process on the branches, making their load a little lighter.

Don't Look Back

Did he turn around one last time and look? Did he take it all in, realizing it was the last time he'd see the house he built, slowly but surely, over the forty-one years he raised his family there? That's what I'd like to know: Did he take one last look?

I'm guessing he did not. I suppose after a day with the moving company—in and out and finally ready, cars and trucks running and ready for the two-and-a-half-hour drive—that he just locked the door and quickly moved to his car. I picture this not because he was in a hurry or couldn't bear to look, but because he was ready to move on, move forward.

Moving forward means being closer to his kids and grandkids. It means moving away from construction and new roads being paved where there was once field and forest. Leaving this place is easier because he learned that the new owners are tree lovers and could challenge him on knowing all the tree names in his beloved forest on his property. Their son is a bird lover and will feed the birds, just like Dad did. Everything has a time and a season.

I went to visit a friend the week before my parents moved from the house they'd lived in for over four decades, where they raised four kids. I hadn't seen her in almost a year, and I'd been invited to her house where she'd recently moved in with her partner. Almost immediately upon entering her kitchen, I saw a china cup and saucer that was identical to my gramma's set. I owned the dinner plates but had never seen the other pieces. It left me with a feeling of absolute comfort and some outer worldliness. My friend said her partner had found it in a box in the garage that the previous owners had left behind. It made me feel that we are all the same. We all move on at some point. We leave our legacy behind for the next people to carry forward—naming the trees, feeding the birds, and displaying things of beauty. The house itself, and the items contained in it, are only pieces of us, not our whole story. Weeks later, my friend brought the teacup and saucer to me as a gift. To think that it was found and wound up in my hand makes me think we have nothing to fear.

He did not look back, I am sure of it.

We All Have a Book in Us

The dishes looked different today. (They seemed happy?) I sure was happy. I'd just realized a dream. I had finished writing a draft of my first book and cover letter and had submitted my "work of art" to a publisher.

Do your dishes look happy? If not, it's likely because you're not happy. The dishes will always be there, and if you're always tending to them, your hobbies and interests will go unnoticed, unknown, and remain hidden.

The dishes weren't looking at me scornfully, with arms crossed, judging why it took me so long to show up. They were saying, "Hi! Welcome and thanks!"

Having trouble losing those extra pounds? Look to your hobbies and interests first. Your mind needs a strong focus on which to anchor itself. Not following our dreams breeds stress, and stress makes us feel that we need a reward or comfort to soothe us. Food fills that need, and rightfully so—we do need to feel healed. Try setting that food aside, even for just a few minutes, and ask yourself what your interests are. Spend some time with these thoughts and see what happens.

Got clutter around you and think you should spend your day cleaning and tidying? It's the same dilemma. The clutter will always be there, and your calling, your true self, right behind it. Let the chores wait. Put yourself and your soul first.

Keep on Marching

I could tell you about how I played the bagpipes at my neighbour and good friend's funeral. About how I hung my head and cried after playing "Amazing Grace." As I did this, I noticed a man, I think his brother-in-law, crying too out there in the cemetery. But that's not the story I'd like to tell you.

This is a story about the bagpipes themselves. I'd taken them in for repair in order to play at the funeral, and remember asking myself why I hadn't played them for so long. How could I have let that slip? The bagpipe repair guy (this does exist, I was happy to find out) deemed the bagpipes potentially salvageable, and we took them to the back room for further inspection. I remember the sound of the clunk of the handle as I set the old case on the table. The bagpipes had been purchased used, and who knows how old they actually were. The young man released the clips on what I now realized was a very ratty case. The case looked foreign under the florescent lights of the repair shop. Some parts of the case were so threadbare, you could almost see right inside to the bagpipes. I re-noticed certain stickers the previous owner must have stuck on there, indicating places he (or she) had traveled with these bagpipes. I now wondered why I hadn't taken them off yet. A denial of ownership of these bagpipes? Not enough time to consider tidying up the outside of their case? Too much introspection? Perhaps.

"How long has it been since you played?" he asked, breaking into my efforts to answer these questions in my mind.

I told him it had been over a year. With a "tisk, tisk" tone that I may or may not have imagined, he investigated the crispiness of the bag part of the bagpipes, at which point he also discovered that it hadn't been seasoned or moisturized during the time I had owned them, which was now ten years.

He concluded that they would need seasoning and a new reed. As we talked, he released to freedom the one drone reed that previously had fallen into the bag part of the pipes, neglected and abandoned until now. As he happily played the chanter to test out the best reed replacement, I could tell he was talented.

When I took the pipes out later to practice for the funeral, I found a note. It said: "Good luck." We were connected by a common love of this instrument.

Several months later I was at a Scottish festival with my family. We were standing at a booth where the vendor was selling bracelets made of precious stones. We'd joined into a conversation already in progress.

"This one is for protection, this one for rejuvenation, this one for courage, and this one for confidence."

I need all those things, I thought. But without enough funds to buy it all, I settled on a black onyx bracelet. Just as I did, the pipe band I used to belong to marched by right behind me. I could feel the breeze from their organized march and the flow as they pushed the air aside for them to play through. I got goosebumps. The merchant explained that black onyx on the bracelet provides a powerful protective force, transforming negative energy and helping to prevent the drain of personal energy. Black onyx aids the development of emotional and physical strength and stamina, especially when support is needed during times of stress, confusion, or grief. It felt right to me, and just what I needed.

It was alright that I hadn't played the bagpipes in so long. I was still able to have them repaired and to play at my friend's funeral and honour him. I was still able to re-connect with my pipe band friends and catch up. Many challenges in life redirect us, and it's important that once healed from some of life's more traumatic experiences, we reflect and re-assess. I've come to realize that there's not just one thing in your life that you're destined to do. It may be many. It may not be large things; they may be or seem small. But all these things add up to who and what you are in this world. Each has equal value to the universe.

Will I pick up the bagpipes again? Will I buy a new case or take someone else's stickers off? Or will I change my focus to writing, or a different instrument, or to just marvel at the evolution of my children as they blossom under my care? Any or all is alright. I suppose all you can do is just keep marching. Keep moving on. One foot in front of the other. Keep investigating with a curious mind what your next focus will be. Things do change, they are different, but all will be alright. Keep searching, keep steady, stay strong.

Little People Love

The kids were getting ready for a dance at the town library, and my husband and I were headed out for a much-needed date. It was one of those nights when you question your motive for temporarily leaving the family nest. It's important to invest time in your relationships, because so much time and energy goes into supporting the kids; however, that night was my son's first dance experience, and I was going to miss his going and returning. In previous years he'd seen his older sister go, not seeming too interested and understanding that he didn't qualify. Now that he could go, he was up for the adventure, and I was proud of him.

When we got home from our date, I went to his room and found him asleep. He somehow knew I was there and asked for a drink. I asked him how the dance was and he said the standard "good." I did the usual ask-as-many-questions-as-you-can routine until you get what you're looking for, and I got it.

"Did you dance?" I asked.

"A little," he answered.

"Did other people dress up in a Halloween costume?"

"Yeah, John had spiked hair and black eyes and lips," he answered appreciatively.

Then the big question. "Was Ashley there?"

"Yes," he said. "She bought me a pop."

How wonderful, I thought, *for the girl he admired to buy him something at the event*. He was quiet for a while, and I thought he was asleep. He rolled over, almost asleep again, and whispered, "I saw her dancing." Then he drifted away for a good night's rest.

These little people really do feel love.

There Is a Place

Let me tell you about a place where time stands still and you forget your worries because happiness fills your heart. This place has beaches, piers, sailboat harbors, and rocks on the beach so large that kids have to move them with both hands. This place has a most beautiful walkway in the woods, which leads to a magnificent waterfall you can swim up to and feel the power of the water as you approach, finally touching it.

I'm not describing this place properly. It sounds busy. It's not. There are large, seemingly endless roads of field upon field of wildflowers, and pastures filled with livestock. Wherever you stand you can see pieces of lake showing through the greenery, because there happens to be approximately one hundred lakes on this island. Nobody's 100 percent sure exactly how many lakes exist, because it's not necessary to know; it's something you feel. Ice cream shops; local artisan crafts like paintings and gift cards; homemade pies and tarts; books by authors whose houses you can drive by; look-outs; a theatre in the woods—all this is at your beck and call. As you drive from one town to another, it's impossible to choose which one you like better—the fields or the harbour and beaches, because each has its beauty. You can sit and ponder this question at an ice cream shop stationed at the side of a country road surrounded by nothing but fields, which will happen to give you one of the most delicious ice cream cones you'll ever have in your life.

Everyone talks to one another here. It's very different from the awkward bus stop gatherings we entertain at home during the kids' school year. This starts on the ferry ride over to the island and continues along our travels. "Where are you from and what brings you here?" These questions aren't asked to be nosy but in recognition of the common bond amongst people on the island, whether visitors, cottagers, or permanent residents. We've all been drawn there for the same reasons, and it's fun to share.

What struck me most on my last visit were the artisans. Our lovely friends and hosts informed us about a water colour painting course for kids offered at the market by the beach that coming Wednesday. My daughter sat and painted what turned out to be a beautiful picture of the large stone building by the beach, which houses my favourite museum on the lower level, and a pottery and stained-glass window store on the second floor. The rest of us wandered around the market while a man played his guitar and sang Willie Nelson and Simon and Garfunkel songs, to name a few. The local artists unabashedly sold their created treasures. It made me remember that this is what it's all about: finding that one creative outlet that is all yours and doing it! Of course, you don't have to sell your creations, but when selling, there's that element of sharing what you do with the world, which may brighten or inspire someone else's day. Some offered art work, others baked goods, wood carvings, note cards, and jewelry. Our friends are in a choir, and we were lucky enough to hear their performance a few days later. The sound that came from the fifteen or sixteen of them rivaled any larger choir from the big city.

A particular lighthouse also caught my attention. When we walked up to it, we assumed that the two large hammocks were for visitors to the lighthouse. We realized later that the hammocks belonged to the people who live there during the summer months. They're carrying on a tradition from two generations back, when their relatives proposed to the coast guard to lease the living space in the lighthouse. In return, they'd maintain the place. Previous to this proposal, the lighthouse was regularly vandalized, as it was unoccupied. The evolution of the battery powered light in the lighthouse eliminated the need for a lighthouse keeper.

This lighthouse isn't one of the more modern ones you often see, with a winding staircase to the top. This one has a kitchen, a living room, and bedrooms. There's an outdoor shower and an outhouse. Every summer our tour guide and her mother come to the lighthouse to tell others about the way it was, and we all appreciate the changes as we compare it to how things are now. The current dwellers tell stories of the past lighthouse keepers who would ride bikes on an uncut trail along the waters' edge and light the lifesaving lamp with kerosene fuel to ensure all vessels were as safe as possible. This cycle would repeat day after day, as it was the only way.

There's a re-typed laminated letter on display that was found in the wall of the lighthouse. It was written by a lighthouse keeper and it stated that Germany had just invaded Poland, and the war had begun. He had just re-wallpapered and was worried about his job security, as kerosene was being replaced by the battery. He mentioned that his heart was failing him. A note underneath his letter let us know that he wound up being the lighthouse keeper for another two years. Somehow that made me feel relieved. We also heard stories from our tour guide of crossings over the ice with sleighs pulled by oxen in the middle of winter to get supplies from the mainland. Some crossings were deadly, as some froze to death in their attempt to cross.

A log book that dates back to 1969 keeps track of visitors and the water. Our tour guide's great grandmother annually tracked each year her earliest and latest swim. She even recorded when she'd dig a hole in the ice in late October to go swimming. I can't imagine doing this, yet it's very intriguing to me.

The people on this island preserve the history well. You can tell it's valued and honoured, perhaps because it's an island—a little harder to reach, but worth the getting to.

Unless

Unless. What a great word. It indicates a possibility that things could be different. It conjures up images of two paths, and your job is to decide what you're going to do. "I should." "I could." "I would." "I will."

Unless.

Acceptance Brings Peace

The night was definitely magical. It was Christmas Eve, when time stands still, when it's all about to happen. Those moments hold the essence of what was, what is now, and what is going to be.

My son and I were outside in the dark, looking up at the night sky and searching for any sign of Rudolph. We saw nothing but stars and planes and colourful Christmas lights surrounding us in the comfort of our neighbourhood.

My son was idly kick-kick-kicking patches of ice stuck hard to the driveway when I noticed our neighbour's light on in his shed. This is a home away from home for him, where he has a few drinks in his heated and moderately-furnished structure out back. Not a cloud in the sky, not an inkling of even a breeze on this starry Christmas Eve, as my son and I made our way to our neighbour's shed.

"Merry Christmas!" we said in unison as I gave him a hug. We exchanged details of our plans for Christmas. He was alone Christmas Eve, but the next day he was headed to a friend's place for a family Christmas dinner.

"Well, you just made my night," he said.

I was impressed with his acceptance of being alone on such a glorious night. He even seemed at peace about it, appreciative of his plans for the next day but still quite alright with his current situation.

Stephanie Malo

I made a mental note to attempt to adopt my neighbour's peace, acceptance, and happiness with what is presented to me each day. My son and I made our way back inside our cozy home to prepare for the dance of sugar plums in our dreams as we awaited the magic that is Christmas.

We All Have a Story

My second book signing was even more successful than the first, if I compare the number of copies sold. I've come to realize that it's not all about how many books I sell, but that it's talking to people that draws me to participate and makes the time fly when I'm there.

"I wish you could write my story," she said.

"What's your story?" I asked, picturing writing it. Her story turned out to be pretty sad and horrifying. She and her husband had been on a motorcycle holiday and had been in an accident. He was killed instantly. She lived for three days in a coma, undergoing operation after operation and not knowing he was gone. She was flown home with her own personal nurse in time to go to her husband's funeral and view the open casket. She was in such bad shape that she almost wasn't able to go. She had to beg the doctors. She began the fight of her life to learn to walk and talk again. She had to rebuild her life without her husband and with disabilities.

She flipped through my book and stopped the sea of pages at the title: "You Are Not Just a Number." She said that, in a sense, we are just a number, because when our number's up, it's up. Her number wasn't up yet, and there she was buying a book about stopping to smell the flowers. We continued to talk about the saying that reminds us that we aren't given any challenge we can't handle. We stood there a moment, pondering that notion, until I confessed that it isn't always an easy one to swallow. She agreed and said she was a bit mad at God for challenging her so much.

I took the opportunity to tell her something that I've only ever told close family members or friends: I've had three visions of loved ones who have passed on. These visions weren't dreams. They all had the same message: Don't cry for them too long. "This" was all good, all amazing, all wonderful, and nothing to worry about. How is this possible? I don't know, but I got the feeling that life after death is much closer than we realize.

"It's like this," I said, bringing my hands together and interfolding my fingers on each hand. "Closer than we could ever imagine, and somehow one and the same."

"I sure hope so," she said. She tucked her copy of the book under her arm and headed towards the in-store coffee shop with her teenage daughter. She asked if she could buy me a coffee, which I desperately needed because I'd forgotten to even eat supper in anticipation of the book signing. She brought the coffee to me as I talked with someone else who had stopped by my table.

Another woman walked by with her mom and laughed at the title. She told me her dog stops to smell each and every flower he walks by. I asked her to send me a picture of this, and she promised that she would.

A lovely young couple stopped to talk, and we all agreed that there's not enough positive in the world. She's going to download the book on her eReader.

A man was intrigued at the title, because his wife is always telling him he needs to stop and smell the flowers. He wanted to get the book for her, but how could he when it was meant for him? I told him they could both read it. He laughed and said he'd think about it. He circled the whole store and came back and got one.

Three people rang the bell in the gift section across from me in the four hours that I was there. Many people walked by the bells and noticed them, but only three of those people thought to pick one up and give it a listen. Why is that noteworthy? I don't know. Maybe each of our lives is like the bell—present every day but needing a leap of faith and a curious mind to ring out and believe.

Selling books is great, but meeting people is even better.

Society

We seem to be doing much better. We hold doors for each and go above and beyond. Yesterday I held a door open for someone behind me. While I waited, a man coming into the store held a door open for me. The woman behind me went through, I kept holding the door for the man, and she held the door for me. At one point only one of the three of us was walking through a doorway. Seems complicated? Well, it wasn't. It was beautiful, and we all laughed. I love that sound.

On another day, we'd been on a big road trip and I was fairly exhausted. It had been a great time, and we were headed home. I had stopped to get gas, and there had been lots of nattering in the car about where we would stop for supper and who likes what and who doesn't. Unbeknownst to me, I had driven off with my gas cap still unhooked, open and dangling. When I stopped at a red light, the guy in the car beside me pointed and motioned to me that my gas cap was open. I nodded a thank you and thought I'd stop and fix it once I turned left. Next, I saw a lady in a pretty white summer dress in my rear-view mirror get out of her car behind me and quickly close my gas cap. She gave me the thumbs up that she'd fixed it and got back into her car. We turned left once the light turned green and I honked a thank you to her. She honked a goodbye back. That's how we look after each other. Keep spreading the good. Keep up the good work.

Observations in the Bushes and Other Life Lessons, by Vicki Bergmann

Through the tall grasses and mounds of leaves came a rustling sound. For some reason, I later thought to name him Parsley the Pig; however, he wasn't a pig at all but a Jack Russell terrier. He was just the right size for a pig, with his furry skin drawn tight over his back. At first a startling sight, he evoked the fight or flight reaction in us as he leapt from his hiding spot and ran circles around us. We had seen him before. His keeper lived next door. His favourite thing to do was to explore in the greenery in the space between her house and ours.

Once we'd said hello to Parsley, he'd run back to his hiding spot, turning to look back at us once or twice along the way to check that we were still sitting there. I'd like to be his friend, but he only quickly responded to a kind good morning and then moved on his way, touring what to him would be a big, green forest.

He appeared to be a combination of bravery and fear as he investigated his surroundings. He gave me hope that those who might have a negative reaction to being surprised by someone or something they're unsure of may still be won over. His actions and personality reminded me that things are not always as they seem, not to judge a book by its cover, and to be open to life's experiences and energies.

The Flight

She was gripping the arms of her chair, white knuckles displaying themselves on a delicate, thin hand. Her jacket was contrastingly tough—a rugged, outdoorsy style coat that made me think she might like hiking, but she was clearly afraid of this plane ride.

She wasn't alone. Where most others seemed alright with what I would describe as extreme turbulence, I gripped my beer instead of the arms of my chair, for fear that my calming fluid would spill. The plane seemed to be alternating between lurching forward and doing some sort of air braking. It was likely due to high winds—nothing the plane couldn't handle, save for a few occupants.

I'm not a frequent flyer, for whatever reason. My job doesn't require it, I never flew much growing up, and I've been busy raising my own family. Back in the day we went on lots of other adventures, like wilderness canoeing, camping, and sailing. All hold their own degree of risk, but because flying is the least commonly experienced thing for me, it's also the most hated and the least understood. I've heard the statistics and know that it's safer to fly than to drive, but my overactive brain can't help but wonder if anyone's applied some sort of equation to the fact that there are so many cars on the road, the sheer volume would account for more mishaps.

Does it matter? So many details, so little time. It brings me to the actual point at hand: vulnerability. Being on a plane reminds me of being buckled into the inside of a tin can and agreeing to fly twenty-thousand-plus feet in the sky to my destination. A long way down if something goes wrong. The burning question is: How long do we have on this earth anyway? What a shame to waste *any* of it.

I wonder how many other people were afraid on the turbulent plane, but I just couldn't tell: reading books, listening to music, drinking wine ... a few sending knowing glances to their friends in the other seats as we seemed to be on a bike ride, rolling up and down hills.

The reward that followed was the time spent in New York City, our destination—an experience that will never be duplicated, simply because we only live once. A play on Broadway, a meditation talk, a Christmas Market at Columbus Circle, and shopping, shopping, and more shopping provided an escape from the everyday. A step back to take an aerial view of my life and reassess.

What about life right now? What about just letting go, hoping for the best, and honouring each life moment? What we have is right now and where we want to go.

The Frog and the Filing Cabinet

My goal was to clean out my filing cabinet, full of twenty years of documents and manuals and paperwork stored for some unknown reason. Maybe it was a "hang on to it just in case" kind of feeling I'd had which made me store it. We were purging, and the next day we'd be taking unwanted stuff to the dump, so it was now or never. While I quickly finished washing the dishes, I heard a chirp. It was so loud, I wasn't sure what it was. It sounded like a bird, but it was dark out so I thought that unlikely. The chirping was so constant, I had to go out and take a look. I followed the sound in an indirect line in the back yard, finally finding the source: a frog. What a discovery! I took a picture of him, as I thought I should document what I was witnessing. I thought of videotaping once the chirping came back, but the frog must have sensed I was there, because it became quiet. It was lodged in between the pool deck and the pool rail. It wasn't stuck; I investigated closely to make sure of that. I waited and waited to hear the sound again, but the frog fell silent. I texted my sister a picture of the frog, telling her about my experience, and headed inside and downstairs to the task at hand.

As I began sorting through the filing cabinet in the basement, I could hear the frog chirping again. My sister texted me back with this:

"As a Celtic symbol meaning, the Frog was deemed lord over all the earth, and the Celts believed it represented curative or healing powers because of its connection with water and cleansing rains. More Western and European views focus on the Frog's three stages of development (egg, tadpole, fully formed amphibian) to symbolize resurrection and spiritual evolution. For these same reasons it is also a common Christian symbol for the holy trinity and resurrection. It is often seen in Christian art to express this symbolism." ~ http://www.spiritcharms.co.uk/index.php?/topic/2087-symbolism-of-the-frog/

Neat, I thought to myself. I focused on the idea of spiritual evolution as I continued the task of sorting papers and documents, revealing to me where I'd been, the paper trail marking my path. The chirping got so loud, it distracted me from my task. I went outside to take a look at it again. When I got close, he stopped the chirping again. I felt the frog was calling me, and then each time I went out, would fall silent. I couldn't even describe to you the wonderful, electric, and eerily life-giving feelings this gave me ... like I was being called. Called to what? Maybe to pay attention, to believe, to feel.

I headed back into the house and closed the kitchen windows to drown out the repetitive sounds. When I returned to the basement, I could still hear him. I wondered what this message for me was. It was then that I found the most interesting paperwork of all—feedback from participants in a course I'd taught some twenty years ago. The comments were beyond complimentary. Some said they enjoyed the course so much, they'd refer others if it was offered again. I read that people enjoyed it so much, they'd take the same course over again to add to their learning. They enjoyed my presentation style, and I made it easy to absorb.

Reviewing this feedback from the course I'd developed and taught brought me a moment of clarity. I knew that I was exactly where I was supposed to be. Not only that, but I have *always* been right where I'm supposed to be. It wasn't a new thing. The light we carry is always our light and our true calling within our spirit. Heavy duty, right? The truth of this rang through as loud as the frog's call.

My Shadow

Losing Aberdeen was like losing my own shadow. She was like a gargoyle always watching over me, looking out for me, and ever silently present. If I went to the basement to do laundry, she waited for me at the top of the basement stairs. If I sat on the front deck late at night to breathe in the night air and look at the moon and the quiet neighbourhood, she waited for me inside, sitting pretty in our entranceway.

When she died, realizing that she was truly gone was like having my heart ripped in two, or the rug pulled out from under me. She was ninety-five human years old. It was time for her. She wasn't well, but the instinct for survival is strong in all animals, including humans. It was her time, but part of me thought she'd go on forever, that she'd be my constant shadow and companion.

It even took me awhile to realize she needed to go to the vet. The cancer progressed as rapidly as my recognition of what was about to happen was slow. The suffering is nasty for the sufferer and the loved ones watching, but somehow it makes everyone ready for the inevitable. The vet said that euthanasia was the last nice thing we could do for our cat. The vet saw her mother suffer with cancer and could do nothing. The vet's secretary called it "the circle of life," as if an announcement to the air around us at that moment, and to the day outside and up to the universe itself, acknowledging not only what I was going through, but also what it means to be alive and gone. The way it is.

Stephanie Malo

We have Angus now. He's a black and white, adorable kitten we rescued. I figured it would be good to show the kids the flip side of life—how it starts out with all its cuteness and youthful energy and happiness. I'm not sure what our other cat, Willamina, thinks, as she's seventeen and a half and set in her ways. Does she miss Aberdeen? Does she wonder if she's next? She's my husband's cat, rescued before my husband and I met. Aberdeen was my rescue. Does Willamina wonder what we've gotten her into when Angus watches her tail wag and tries to pounce on it? Angus will approach us, looking for a pat on the head or back, and then just before contact will scootch away, just beyond reach. He does it to every family member. I wasn't sure I had the capacity to love another cat until one day Angus was missing and I feared his little furry body had fallen down the sump pump we'd forgotten to cover. It was then I realized that this cat is important to me and to our family.

You see, the heart can heal with time … with the knowledge that your "lost" loved one wants you to be happy, and that all is good in this very moment. Know this and believe in it.

Keep on Believing

I stood there with her in the hallway, a safe hearing distance away from her brother. I stared deep into her eyes, hoping that the longer and deeper I stared, the greater the chance I wouldn't have to answer her question. I was hoping for an explosion or an equally interesting distraction to keep me from telling her the truth. Because the truth would take my daughter from the innocence of childhood to the knowledge of an adult. She had asked me if Santa was real.

She'd asked me this four or five times over the course of the last two or three weeks, and I'd managed to avoid the inevitable. But now I realized it had only been a temporary reprieve. She told me some kids at school don't believe in Santa—that he's not real. At the time, I'd cleverly answered, "What? Really? So these kids don't put stockings out? I feel bad for them, because if you don't believe, you don't receive!"

But this time was different. When she asked me in the hall, she was pale and wore a panicked look on her face. I could feel my body slinking down the wall, ever so slowly, like I was having trouble supporting myself. Staring into her searching eyes, with no distraction available to avert her attention, I shook my head and answered "no."

How would I explain to her the value of tradition, how my mother and my mother's mother and so on had held to this tradition? How this tradition helps you believe in that which you cannot see? That it teaches of heart-felt giving and that people are capable of bringing joy to others. That St. Nicholas *was* a saint, that there was a person, that there is a process to determining sainthood, that all of this rolled together can far surpass whether or not Santa exists. Where would I start?

I started with one statement: that this whole Santa thing, this technically strange and eventually disappointing belief in Santa, actually teaches wonder.

A few nights later as I was tucking her into bed, this all truly sank in for her.

"Mom," she said, "are you sure that there's no Santa?"

"Did I tell you too soon?" I asked.

"No," she answered with a now discernibly grown up looking face. She confided that she already suspected.

"Why don't you just keep believing? That's what I do."

She really liked that notion—that her mom, and maybe her mom's mom, still look up at the night sky on Christmas Eve to try to catch a glimpse of Santa and his reindeer bringing the magic of Christmas to all.

In Stillness We Find Life

Leave it to my younger sister to find the prettiest cemetery ever. She's all about beautiful paintings and bedspreads and colours. Stuff to draw the eye—beauty. She went and did it again when she chose the cemetery for her daughter, who was born too early and only lived for one day. There are other graves there, of course. Others only lived for one day, some two days, some two weeks, one two years. Stuffed animals had been left at some grave sites, and one even had pink flip flops beside the grave, probably in the size they would have needed at this point in time if they had still been here. Speaking of time, it stands still here today as I observe all this—not in a creepy or sad way. Somehow the energy is positive. Love surrounds the place, as well as an acceptance that not all (or many) things turn out as planned. The birds' chirping is exceptionally clear. I wonder if it's due to the fact that there are no busy streets nearby, and this cemetery is tucked away from the hustle and bustle.

I found the cemetery by accident today, although I'd been there once before. I instructed my cell phone GPS to get me to my appointment, so when it led me here, I knew I needed to come back once I'd accomplished my morning goals. Messages set by the graves by moms, dads, grammas and grandpas, and siblings show more of a state of peace than sadness or suffering. One in particular sticks with me, stating that if only with us for a day, it was enough to teach us to love, and comforts us is in the knowledge that an angel is protecting from above.

Rise

I'll always remember the day I turned forty. I'm not sure why we decided to launch it in the back yard by the pool … probably because there was lots of water available, in case we needed to extinguish the flame and abort mission. There we were, my husband and I, holding the paper sky lantern and waiting patiently for it to fill with carbon dioxide from the flame and hopefully rise on its own. *Will it work?* we wondered, as we thought about what we were going to wish for.

We tried to let go of it a few times, but it wasn't ready. It wobbled and gently floated back to our waiting, steadying hands. Finally, we felt it lift, stronger and with more conviction than it had before. Ever so slowly it started to rise. It hovered close to the crab apple tree, almost as if taking a closer look, and then went on its way. We watched as it approached our neighbour's giant maple tree, our hearts beating fast, hoping it wouldn't get tangled and knowing there was the potential of the small flame starting a fire. We held hands and ran from the back yard to the front and down the driveway in time to see our lantern friend clear the tree and cross the road, rising higher and higher. It gained speed and within seconds faded in the distance, glowing all the way, farther and farther until the tiny speck of light vanished and went out.

I asked my husband what he wished for, and he said another forty years. Cheers to the future and endless possibilities.

The Dance of Life

*One would have liked to have taken chances,
but not recklessly;
Loved much,
without losing one's self;
Held true to values,
while being open to learn new ways;
Been neat and tidy,
without it taking over your life;
Taken time to be in the moment,
while still having goals for the future;
Given time, money, and help as often as possible,
even if there was not a lot extra;
Tried our best,
because in the end, that's all we can do, is try.
Good Luck.
Wishing you all the best,*

Stephanie

Acknowledgments

First of all, thank you to the public library in my town (and sometimes in the neighbouring town) for being my place of solace and quiet (and not always quiet). Gosh, what would we all do without libraries? Such a communal place to learn and read and investigate. I love it there so much, I wrote some stories about it!

Theresa, thank you for your proofreading skills and effort. Most of all, thank you for telling others you were proofreading the book. As you told people how some of the stories made you tear up, I knew you were proud of me and valued my skills and intentions. I'm proud of you too.

Elaine, thank you also for your proofreading skills and effort. I appreciate how you "get it" and understand my goals for writing these stories, how you said you were careful with your editing suggestions as you didn't want to inadvertently change the tone or the message of the story – that some things were better left with an open ending for the reader to interpret. I know you will one day find your creative calling too.

Andrew, you understand my need to write and publish, because you have your own creative outlet with your music. What a privilege for us to be able to follow our dreams, and what an honour that our dreams bring joy to others.

To my daughter, you are the source of many stories in Stopping to Smell the Flowers. Thank you for putting up with my regular visits to the library, and keeping an eye on your brother in order for me to do so. It is hard to believe you were so little when I wrote the first book. Now you have evolved to a young lady and I know by the third book you will have evolved even more. You are a special gift and I treasure every day with you.

To my son, you are also the source of many stories in the books I write. Thank you for putting up with my regular visits to the library on Saturday mornings and into the early afternoon. Thanks for dropping in occasionally to the library to visit me as you rode your bike around town - for being interested in what makes me happy and where my creative writing takes place. You make my heart sing.

Mallory, you were the one who said, "I see a trilogy here, a box set", and well, because of that, it is underway. I love our conversations, and consider myself lucky that we get to visit almost daily. As my daughter says "You've got Mallory."

Thank you to those who told me they read the first *Stopping to Smell the Flowers*: Extraordinary Observation of Everyday Life twice; who bought multiple copies of it as they had given the book to others to read and never got it back; who put it on their list of top ten favourite books of all time (true story); who told me which story was their favourite; who promoted me and told people in their circles about the book I had written; who put the book on their store shelves; who bought copies for friends, family and co-workers or told me to keep writing (Mom (Vicki), Dad (Roger), Andrew, Theresa, Brad, Steve, Jean, Meg, Jenn, Dan, Ted, Suenya, Chrissy, Christine, Pat, Sherry, Tom, Amanda); who asked when the next book was coming out; who said "How can you write a book about me without even knowing me?" allowing me to answer, "Because we are all the same". In doing so, you all gave me the courage to continue writing and present this next book to you. The third book in the series is on the way. This creating can be contagious and addicting.

Writing is an artform. Art is a basic form of communication. Stories give the reader a visual or an idea or a feeling. They can create a shift in someone, a new way of thinking or seeing, spark an idea, or change a life. I've met my calling if at the very least, I've made my own life better, happier, with the process of writing and creating. Writing brings me joy, and I know for a fact that joy is contagious and the world needs more of it. When we do things that make us happy, those around us pick up that happiness or vibe and then those around *them* pick it up and so goes the ripple effect.

To those who are waiting for the right time to write their book, to paint, to sew, to create: wait no longer. Surround yourself with cheerleaders who will encourage you and get it done. Find your source of joy today and begin. You won't regret it.

Go out. Go out into the woods. You might just find yourself. Go out. Go out into the woods.

Categories

Solitude

A Break from the To-Do-List	pg. 17
The Wind	pg. 19
The Chair in the Woods	pg. 21
Take Time Out	pg. 67
Sure, I'll Go	pg. 83
Acceptance Brings Peace	pg. 109
In Stillness We Find Life	pg. 127

Rest & Recharge

We Don't Claim the Land, We Belong to It	pg. 1
Stopping to Smell the Flowers Isn't Always Easy	pg. 15
Keep Your Vacation with You All Year Round	pg. 29
The Cottage	pg. 59
The Art of Being Present	pg. 73
Spread Your Wings	pg. 75
There Is a Place	pg. 103

Lost & Found

Retracing Your Roots	pg. 51
Life Coming to a Halt	pg. 55
Light in the Darkness	pg. 65

Don't Look Back   pg. 93

Purpose

Purpose   pg. 47
The Library   pg. 49
Imprints   pg. 87
Unless   pg. 107
We All Have a Story   pg. 111
The Flight   pg. 119

Synchronicity & Symbolism

Choices   pg. 9
Talk to Me, Honey Bee   pg. 79
The Frog and the Filing Cabinet   pg. 121

Hobbies & Interests

On Following Your Dreams   pg. 11
Time on My Hands   pg. 13
Comfort from Books   pg. 33
We All Have a Book in Us   pg. 95
Keep On Marching   pg. 97

Relationships

This Time by Choice   pg. 5
The Funny Thing About Being a Parent   pg. 23
Practicing Paying It Forward   pg. 25
No Regrets   pg. 27

Facing the Stuff as Time Moves On	pg. 39
Blinking Lights	pg. 41
On Being Happy	pg. 45
Teaching Fear by Accident	pg. 57
On Letting Go	pg. 63
Evolving	pg. 69
The Jog of My Life	pg. 71
The Baby Shower	pg. 89
Little People Love	pg. 101
Society	pg. 115
Observations in the Bushes and Other Life Lessons	pg. 117
My Shadow	pg. 123
Keep on Believing	pg. 125

Presence

One Foot in Front of the Other	pg. 35
BBQ and Meditate	pg. 43
Content	pg. 61
Right Where We're Supposed to Be	pg. 77
Blessings Raining Down	pg. 85
The Sounds of Silence	pg. 91
Rise	pg. 129

About the Author

Stephanie lives near London, Ontario, Canada with her husband, two children and four cats. She plays the bagpipes when she remembers to, writes at the local library every week and has a full-time career in sales and marketing. She guides a mindfulness meditation group in her community which has quickly grown in membership and has expanded to two additional locations, showing there is a need for people to carve out space to stop and consider their lives for a moment and to wake up from the trance in which we can find ourselves. Stephanie is the author of Stopping to Smell the Flowers: Extraordinary Observations of Everyday Life. She is currently working on the third book in the Stopping to Smell the Flowers series.

Also by Stephanie Malo
Stopping to Smell the Flowers:
Extraordinary Observations of Everyday Life

www.ingramcontent.com/pod-product-compliance
Lightning Source LLC
Jackson TN
JSHW081444130925
90923JS00005B/145